A Pot Mess

Journals of a Royal Navy Cook

Leading Cook J.A. Parker.

A Pot Mess

Journals of a Royal Navy Cook

by

J.A. Parker

The Memoir Club

First published in 2000 by
The Memoir Club
Whitworth Hall
Spennymoor
County Durham

British Library Cataloguing in
Publication Data.
A catalogue record for this book
is available from the
British Library.

ISBN: 1 84104 014 2

Typeset by George Wishart & Associates, Whitley Bay.
Printed by Bookcraft (Bath) Ltd.

Contents

Dedicated
to my wife Pauline

List of Illustrations

Foreword

by Malcolm Clarke, Chairman of HMS Solebay Association

Throughout the history of the Royal Navy the work of the cooks has largely gone unrecorded. They often worked in difficult conditions – cooking a three-course meal for two hundred people while the kitchen is seesawing up and down and rolling from side to side is not something that I would relish. Coping with the vagaries of weather and sometimes substandard ingredients, the ship's cooks made sure that the ship's company received three hot meals a day, fresh bread when the nearest baker was a few hundred miles away, and a varied diet. In small ships, the lone cook could have a significant effect on morale and efficiency. In ships of any size, the galley was important to the health and wellbeing of the ship's company. As a young sailor during the Suez landings, I well remember the efforts made to keep us fed while we were at action stations, even though half the galley staff were themselves closed up at guns or in ammunition rooms.

This memoir covers a time when the Royal Navy was very different to the Royal Navy of today. Living conditions were more basic, with men sleeping in hammocks or on benches, 20 or 30 to a mess. Messdecks were multi-role, serving as sleeping, eating and recreational spaces. I still have a photograph somewhere of breakfast aboard *Solebay* with some people eating at the table while others stand on the same table unslinging their hammocks. The requirements of the service in those days were also greater. It was quite normal for a ship to serve on a foreign station for 12 to 18 months 'unaccompanied', i.e. wives remaining in the UK. The working week was 5½ days, and uniform was invariably required when going ashore. This is in stark contrast to modern conditions, where messes are smaller, where eating is done in central dining halls, and where service away from the home port is seldom more than a few months. Even as I write this, there is an article in *Navy News* saying what a strain it will be for a ship going on a seven-month deployment. The catering has changed considerably, with multiple choices of menu replacing the single 'choice'. Galleys are more sophisticated, and the distinction between officers and ship's cooks has disappeared. So too has the rating of Cook. Jack always avoided using this term anyway, preferring to call them 'Chefs' – now the Navy has taken the hint and 'Chef' has become the official rating.

Mr Parker joined the Royal Navy at a time when conditions were beginning to change as the Service trimmed down and modernised. His experiences ranged from one of the last coal-fired ships to one of the first post-war destroyers, and encompassed shore-duty at a large training establishment. It was a time when conditions on most ships were still very basic, and when the Royal Navy had a world-wide presence. A copious letter writer, he chronicled his daily experiences in letters home. We are fortunate that his wife kept all the correspondence, because it is from these letters that the present book has emerged. They provide a picture of the daily life of the 'Chef', his relationship with colleagues and other members of the ship's company, and his leisure. I enjoyed reading the draft, and I'm sure that many will enjoy the memories that these pages stir.

CHAPTER I

H.M.S. *Solebay*, My First Ship

I JOINED THE NAVY ON 1st February, 1949 and after doing my preliminary training at H.M.S. *Royal Arthur*, went on to H.M.S. *Ceres*, the Naval Cookery School at Harrogate. Then on for a further spell of training to H.M.S. *Pembroke* at Chatham and then back to H.M.S. *Royal Arthur*. That completed my initial training and on 13th July I was drafted to H.M.S. *Solebay*, a Battle Class Destroyer then attached to the Home Fleet. She had been built by Hawthorn Leslie at Hebburn-on-Tyne, launched in 1944 and completed in 1945. From completion until 1953 she was Leader of the 5th Destroyer Flotilla, Home Fleet, and was finally broken up in 1967. I joined her as Assistant Cook. I served on *Solebay* for a year, which seemed to be the normal spell for most members of the ship's company. I now believe she was the type of ship in which experienced sailors used to teach the ropes to green hands such as I myself then was. At the end of my year I just got a draft back to RNB. Probably if I had put in a request to stay on her, it would have been granted, but at the time I did not know whether such a thing was allowed. As a current member of the *Solebay* Association, I now realise that some served for two years.

The Captain had been on board since commissioning and his wife was American. She used to meet him everywhere we went and her car was always the first to arrive at each port of call. When a Captain comes aboard he is always piped, with the Gangway Party, the Officer of the Watch and the Chief Coxswain and his Piping Party all standing to attention. The Captain's wife was always just behind the Captain and as she stepped aboard she used to say 'Hiya, fellers', which invariably produced a smile.

The galley was all-electric and was situated at the break in the fo'c'sle round the funnel, so that part of it was on the port side and part on the starboard. The entrance was near the boiler-room hatch and the deck inside the galley was always warm and often 'bloody hot'. It ruined my feet for ever.

The Chief Cook's name was Swaffer and he lived at Sheerness. If he gave you a blast for something you had done wrong, he would stand near you and give you a shower at the same time. Because the deck was permanently at a temperature ranging from warm to hot, we used to clean it with Bluebell.

H.M.S. Solebay.

After a while that deck, which had steel strips on it to prevent us from slipping, was absolutely shining. One day we noticed the Chief Cook chipping with his finger nail at one of the junction mains boxes. He was trying to see whether it was brass and of course it was. The upshot was that all the boxes, switches and any square box that was attached to the bulkhead had the paint stripped off them and the brass laid bare. From then on we were using more Bluebell than ever! So far as the Chief Cook was concerned, a galley with painted boxes was just not on. For all that, he was quite a decent chap in a way. He had his own laws and would ask a wrongdoer: 'Which do you want, the Officer of the Watch's or my punishment?' His punishment invariably took the form of extra work and you knew where you stood with him. Furthermore he would not allow anything to be said against his staff.

When the 'Pipe Hands to Dinner' used to go at sea, it always seemed to clash with a manoeuvre which called for 'Hard over' to port or starboard. This had a disastrous effect on the food we had been preparing. The worst times of all were when they fired the torpedo tubes on the starboard side. The hot lockers, with all the meals in trays for the messes, were on the port side and there were over twenty messes with at least two trays to a mess. If the lockers were left, all the doors would be flung open and the trays would come sliding out. The only way we found to prevent this happening was for all of us chefs, Chief Cook included, to sit on the deck, each with both his feet pressed on a door and his back against the bulkhead. In fact it was difficult to remain standing anywhere when the tubes were fired.

The Gunnery Officer was always in the galley. he had risen through the Lower Deck and knew all the dodges. If he was Duty Officer when you were going ashore, your turnout had to be a hundred percent. He would send men back in droves for such details as shoes not properly polished, collars or cap tops not up to standard etc.

As I have said, H.M.S. *Solebay* was attached to the Home Fleet. Soon after I joined her we went on a cruise during which our first port of call was St. Nazaire in the Bay of Biscay. The Second World War had ended only a few years before and at this port we could still see where the U-Boats had been housed under no less than sixteen feet of concrete. These U-Boat shelters had been blown up and the enormous mounds of concrete rubble could still be seen. We were doing a series of exercises with the American Sixth Fleet and in the course of these we called at Setubal near Oporto in Portugal. Here we were conducted on a tour of the wine lodges. At this time we were accompanied by H.M.S. *St. Kitts*, our Half-Leader, and also by H.M.S. *Sluys* and H.M.S. *Cadiz*, which made up all of the Fifth Destroyer Flotilla.

One Sunday a group of us decided to make the journey from Setubal to Lisbon. Just after midday we caught a bus and spent a thoroughly good time enjoying the sights of the ancient city. However, we left it rather late to return and were further delayed by having to catch a ferry. By the time we arrived at the bus depot, we found that the last bus had gone so we all gathered in a café and tried to scrape together enough money to 'phone the ship. There were fifteen or twenty of us and when at last we got through, we were told to hire a coach. This we did, though we knew that it would be far from cheap. The distance between Lisbon and Setubal is quite considerable and it took us 2½ hours to get back. At the time the ship paid for the coach and eventually the price was deducted from our pay.

While we were at Setubal a tragic accident occurred, resulting in the deaths of six officers. They were driving together in a car which missed its course and went over the edge of the harbour. The driver was the British Naval Attaché, Commander Cheyne, and we ourselves lost our First Lieutenant, Lieutenant-Commander Ponsonby. The *St. Kitts* also lost her First Lieutenant, while the *Sluys* lost her G/N Officer and two Lieutenants. We had the sad duty of taking the bodies to be buried at Lisbon, and I remember seeing four of the coffins lying on our torpedo tubes. We had been under sailing orders at the time of the accident but of course these arrangements delayed us for a week.

After Setubal we proceeded to Gibraltar, where we met up with the

Mediterranean Fleet and combined with them in further exercises. While here, we had a good run ashore. Some of us climbed the Rock and saw the famous Barbary apes at close quarters. We ended up with a few drinks at the Embassy Bar.

After this we took part in an exercise with submarines, and then called at Casablanca for a few days. The entire flotilla was moored stern to, which meant that we were all in line with our backsides to the harbour wall. As I had no money to spare, I did not go ashore.

From there we continued to Oran, where the stink was so strong that we could smell it before we saw it. Here too we were moored stern to. While at Oran I had a rather strange experience. As always while in harbour, all our gash was put in bins ashore. We used to have rather large tins of Australian fruit and they were well packed in wooden boxes. Off I went one night to find the bins, with two of these boxes filled with empty tins. I found the bins against a wall but just as I was about to put my boxes in them, there was a flurry of robes in the shadows and in a flash I found myself relieved of my boxes and tins and the occupier of the robes making a speedy exit with them to the other side of the wall, his robes still flapping in the evening breeze.

One day while we were at sea an Albatross flew too low across us and got caught in our wires. It landed on the deck stunned but not particularly injured. For the next few days the welfare of the bird figured in Daily Orders! Every morning the first thing we used to do after Reveille was to make our way to the 'heads'. One morning a group of us was in them and about in mid-stream when what should come waddling out of one of the toilets but the Albatross! What a size it was! Its head was level with my shoulder and then those grey eyes looking straight down its beak! It was that hooked beak that really got us bothered. However, it did not show any aggression towards us. Nevertheless, it used to take the entire Duty Watch to move it about the deck. On this occasion we all made a hurried exit from the heads and it was reminiscent of those old Laurel and Hardy films in which three or four people try to get through a door at the same time. I was in the middle! The Albatross was eventually coaxed out and somehow got on to the X Gun Deck, where it eventually flew off. It had remained with us for nearly a week.

An old photograph which I still possess brought back memories of the times when 'Hands to Bathe' was piped. One hot weekend we had come to the end of an exercise earlier than usual. The Flotilla had split up and each ship was on her own, 'showing the flag'. It was a gorgeous afternoon, typical of the Med., with the sea calm as a millpond. I had been on duty all morning and was now off watch. The pipe 'Hands to Bathe Starboard Side' came during the First Dog Watch. It was the first time I had heard this pipe. Now it might be thought that there was nothing to it. The routine was always the same. The gangway used to go down, and sometimes (though not on this particular occasion) a boat was lowered. The order to go in was usually given once everything was in place. There we were, all lined up on the starboard side. 'In you go!' came the shout. I dived in and headed straight out. Ah that wonderful cool water! I cut a swathe through the virgin oggin but after a while I started thinking, 'Why am I on my own?' I stopped, trod water and turned round. 'Bloody hell!' I said to myself, 'I don't think I should be here at all! What's that boat going backwards and forwards from bow to stern for, even though the gangway is still down? I didn't realise how far out I was; I had better get back!' All this flashed through my mind in a matter of seconds, so I started putting my utmost effort into swimming. After a few minutes I was finding the going desperately hard and I felt I was not getting anywhere. Then panic set in and, to be completely honest, I believe I have never been so frightened in my life. I prayed over and over again as I felt my strength going and a terrible weakness creeping over me and still I was failing to make much headway. Eventually I got back amongst the lads. By this time the motorboat was at the bow and turning, and it was at that point that I saw an A.B. by the Coxswain with a rifle in his hands. Even then I had to ask myself: 'Why has he got a rifle? Surely there are no sharks in the Med.?' By this time I was dodging the divers and the idiots who were still jumping in from the fo'c'sle. I had reached the gangway and it was time to get back on board. Suddenly I thought: 'I bet I shall be in the First Lieutenant's Report for this.' At the top of the gangway I saw the Coxswain standing. 'Right lads,' he said calmly enough, 'In the showers.' On seeing me he asked: 'All right, Chef?' That was all. So as soon as we reached the bathroom, we all had a water fight. By this time it was teatime and still nothing had happened and I had not been piped for. No one ever said anything about it. It was many years afterwards that someone explained to me that I had been caught in an undertow and that if I had swum either to left or right, I would have got out of it.

That night I was lying in my hammock thinking how lucky I had been. I had missed the First Lieutenant's Report and not only that, I had avoided being put in the rattle because nobody had seen me. That made me sweat a bit. At evening quarters that night the Chief Cook would have been most annoyed!

Our next port of call was St. Tropez on the French Riviera. Once again the flotilla broke up and spread out over the whole extent of the Riviera, each ship taking its own course. We were anchored out of harbour and had

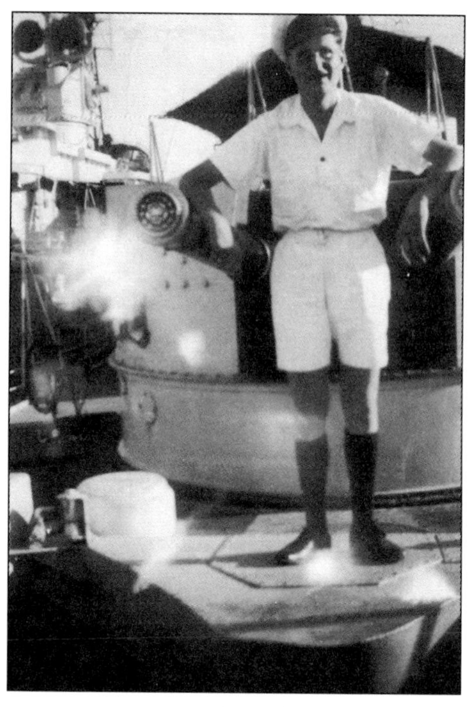

At school again – short pants!

no pay that week, and the town was some distance down the road. One Sunday the Senior Hand, a two-badge A.B., said: 'I am taking the whaler out this afternoon. Do you want to come sailing?' 'Yes,' I replied, so he told me that there would be eight of us and that I should organise some tea. I did this and the same thing was to happen again later. It must have been a regular thing for a party of seamen to include a cook in their number as a way of ensuring that they had a good meal with them. Incidentally, the Two-Badge A.B. was on the *Eskimo* during the War when she received an S.O.S. signal. She went to rescue the ship in trouble at full speed but then she hit a mine and had her bow blown right off. She went straight down. He was on the upper deck at the time and was washed over the side with a few others who survived.

To return to our trip in the whaler. We had a smashing time, sailing up and down the coast and putting in to swim in secluded coves. We were all surprised to see how clear the water was and how well we could see the bottom. We found a marvellous bay with a sandy beach and decided to stop there for tea. We passed a sign that must have read: 'No Admittance. Nudist Colony', but none of us could read French. We couldn't understand why everyone was running away when there were only eight of us. I have never seen so many wobbly bottoms in all my life!

After leaving *Solebay* I stayed for a time in RNB Chatham, one part of which was called St. Mary's. That was where I first met Ken North and we became very good pals. I lived at Market Deeping near Peterborough and since it was a considerable distance from Chatham, I was not able to take all my weekend leaves, so stayed in the RNB. Ken, like myself, was the only son of his family and, realising my position, he asked me to go home with him for weekends to Lewisham in North London. His mother and father were very good to me and we always went out together, sometimes to football matches, sometimes up to the City. His father was an electrician on the Underground at Baker Street Station and worked with the father of a girl we came to know named Pauline. She was a shorthand typist working at the Amalgamated Press in the City and was involved in legal work. Her home was at Eastcote, Middlesex, on the Piccadilly Metropolitan Line to Uxbridge. It was quite close to Wembley Stadium and Harrow on the Hill, where we eventually got married. She too was a friend of the North family. For some reason Ken and she were not really interested in one another in a romantic sense, though Pauline used to treat him like a brother. Then I came along! At first the three of us used to go everywhere together, but then Ken found a girl friend, with the result that for a time we became a foursome. Eventually Ken got a draft to H.M.S. *Rocket* and we rather lost touch with each other. By this time I had joined the *Barcarole* but I was still spending part of my leaves at Mrs North's. Ken and I usually managed to spend these parts of our leaves together.

Pauline and I were now courting but her mother had proved rather possessive. While she was quite happy with seeing her occasional boy friends, she did not know how to handle an engagement. Her father, on the other hand, was quite different and we used to get on pretty well. Under the circumstances we had to be patient and it all took time, but eventually the light dawned.

We had been courting for about eighteen months when one day I said to Pauline: 'Meet you next weekend at Baker Street and we will get that engagement ring.' We had arranged to go to Bravingtons, which was just across the road from Baker Street Station.

The next weekend there I was sitting on Baker Street Station, and although we had arranged the time of our meeting, Pauline was two hours late. It turned out that she had been under pressure and also that she had been doing some deep thinking as to what engagement and marriage meant. Anyway, once she turned up, we went across the road and I bought the ring she wanted. That was fifty years ago!

CHAPTER II

With H.M.S. *Barcarole* in the Scottish Islands and Lochs

I JOINED H.M.S. *BARCAROLE* at Aultbea on 30th October, 1952. We were at Tolsta Head, Isle of Lewis, working on a floating steel pontoon. This was a 'hush-hush' device, the exact nature and purpose of which were secret. The older seamen, who had been with the *Barcarole* for some years, believed that it was a floating laboratory. To keep the device in position, we worked out of Aultbea Boom Defence Base carrying pyramid-shaped concrete clumps to lay on the seabed.

One afternoon while working there, the Captain could not take his bearing from the land because the wooden posts serving as landmarks had fallen down. Since we were short of hands at that particular time, I was roped in to make up a boat's crew of three, and we rowed over and climbed up the rocky headland. There we found the fallen posts and re-erected them without difficulty in their original positions.

At one of the small beaches at Tolsta Head a unique and fascinating geographical phenomenon can be observed. It is full of rolling boulders which make it quite impossible to land there. The whole beach seems to be moving, and the boulders, which are of all sizes, are completely round. In winter the constant gales in these parts bring down the rocks of the headland and the continuous pounding of the waves rounds them off. Eventually they must grind themselves into sand.

One of the lads in the boat told us that the old sailing ships used them as ballast. This raised the question of danger money. Anyone attempting to get them would have found himself with stumps where his feet should be!

During the summer of 1952 we remained working at Aultbea, coaled ship at Ullapool and made occasional trips to Stornoway for a run ashore. One day when we were on our way to Stornoway, we met the tug *Hengest* with the pontoon. Our Captain decided that we would take it over and bring it to Stornoway ourselves. So we made it fast with wires fore and aft along the starboard side. Although the pontoon was a little longer than we were, it seemed to be no trouble.

In that corner of the west coast a storm can blow up quite quickly, and that is exactly what happened. The pontoon was slightly convex, forming

H.M.S. Barcarole – *the ship's company.*

what might be described as a camber deck, and at first it was not easy to see where the wires were secured to it. To make sure that it remained secure, the First Lieutenant was asked to stand on the pontoon so as to keep an eye on the fastenings. There he was, making his way from forrard to aft and trying to keep steady on a heaving camber deck with no guard rail. After a while the Buffer came up, poked his head into the galley, and said: 'Chef, give the First Lieutenant a hand on the pontoon. You keep aft while the First Lieutenant stays forrard'. So there I was, watching that the wire on the after section didn't come loose. A number of hatches on the pontoon were locked and bolted and there was one door, which was the only fixture on the upper deck.

As time went on it became quite frightening. We on the pontoon were going up when the *Barcarole* was coming down and really thumping the side (The Chief ERA's cabin was wrecked but we never got holed). Eventually, as we were coming into Stornoway, we were ordered off the pontoon and both of us were pleased to comply. Then – horror of horrors! – the Harbour Master refused us entry and we were forced to find shelter elsewhere.

The manner in which we had attached the pontoon caused some concern, but in the end it all turned out quite well. We took it up to Tolsta Head and secured it to the buoys, which, in turn, were attached to the clumps.

During this time we were also working on the Boom and on similar jobs.

The Boom was an underwater net used in time of war to prevent submarines from entering the harbour. A Boom Defence Vessel would be in attendance to open a gate in the net for ships to enter or leave, and to close it after them.

The First Lieutenant of *Barcarole* used to do a lot of fishing. One evening I was busy with supper in the galley and was frying fish and chips. The First Lieutenant was opposite the galley door with his rod and tackle. Suddenly he shouted 'Chef, grab this!' and a small plaice came flying into the galley on his line. I quickly removed it from the hook, and after taking the head off and gutting it, I washed and cleaned it, dressed it in flour and batter, and within seconds I had it in the fryer. When it was cooked and nicely browned, I put it on a plate with a knife and fork and handed it to the First Lieutenant saying, 'Impossible to get fish any fresher than this, Sir.'

At one time we were in dry dock aft of the *Tenacious*. A story about a new First Lieutenant on that ship quickly reached us. He had joined the ship a few weeks before and had somehow upset the ship's company. On one occasion a party had gone ashore and, after having a few drinks, were coming back on board during the early hours. They decided to throw pieces of angle iron into the drydock, the sides of which were built in a step formation, each step being about three feet deep. The angle irons happened to be of exactly that length, and the men returning were trying to balance each angle iron on the edge before letting it go so as to make it hit every step down as it fell – all this in the early hours!

The First Lieutenant was waiting with the Duty Watch and when they finally got on board he lined them up. After giving vent to a torrent of invective at their conduct, he tried to discover who the ringleaders were. 'Step forward the ratings who threw those angle irons into the dry dock?' he ordered, 'The rest will then be dismissed.' Not a movement, not a sound! They just stood there, swaying in the breeze. After a while the First Lieutenant said 'We can stay here all night, you know. So who put the angle irons in the dock? One pace forward!' Up piped a Glaswegian voice from the back: 'It's Scott.' Like a flash the First Lieutenant replied, 'Step forward, Scott, now!' Not a movement. 'Which one of you is Scott?' asked the First Lieutenant. 'Scott bugger all to you,' retorted the voice from the back.

It was the 17th August, 1953. I had been on leave and was rejoining my ship at Greenock, (where we were coaling ship) before sailing for Aultbea. It was pouring with rain when I finally got on board, but fortunately I was in time for my tot. The painting of the galley had nearly been finished with the deck-head in white and the bulkhead yellow below a blue border. There were only two others on board and there were no cigarettes to be had as the

First Lieutenant would not issue any. I had brought a portable wireless from home and had rigged it up in the galley with an outside aerial picking up ships in the dock and most stations. The small freshwater tank above the skylight in the galley was being filled, but there was so much pressure in the hose that it shot out and half-drowned me, putting out the fire in the range and flooding the galley.

At about nine one morning we arrived at Loch Ewe in a rough force 7 wind. We still had about eight weeks' work to do at Aultbea on the boom and also on the pontoon moorings at Tolsta Head, Stornoway. That day it was too rough to carry out any work on the boom.

A few days later we sailed for Stornoway, first calling at Ullapool. We would not be coming back to Aultbea until September 31st.

As for our mail, we might be lucky and get it brought to us by the M.F.V. owned by the Boom Defence Base. On arriving at Stornoway, we would be anchoring off the pier because of the state of the tides over the next month. When alongside, we used to go aground and that could be dangerous; the cables would take too much strain.

As we went alongside at Ullapool, a gale blew up and we wrenched a bollard off the pier. From then onwards we were not popular, and later, when we were here for the Coronation, the harbour authorities made it obvious that we were not wanted. The only entertainment available to us was what we devised for ourselves.

The next day we sailed for Stornoway, arriving at 4 p.m. to await orders to take the pontoon off. The following morning the *Hengest*, a sea-going tug, was to take over and then we would be picking up the moorings, anchors, clumps and cables.

We anchored offshore, close to the pontoon, but it was too rough to work on it. Next morning there was still a big swell, so we put in to Stornoway and had a run ashore, going to a barn dance that night. I became ill with a temperature and when I went ashore to see the Doctor, he diagnosed tonsillitis and wanted to send me to hospital. However, that proved impossible because there was no bed to spare.

It was choppy here in the bay, but at 8.30 we were out to the pontoon again. This time we were going to let *Hengest* take it from us but we had to wait for calm weather for the changeover. The chef of the *Hengest* came aboard, hoping to persuade me to exchange with him, but I didn't want a sea-going tug. Her crew had only been ashore five times in three months. Apart from this, Chatham would have had to be informed and could have turned the arrangement down. In any case, the ship's company on *Hengest* was not so good as the one on *Barcarole*.

We had been working on the pontoon all day and finally handed it over to *Hengest* to tow back to Chatham. After that we picked up the moorings and clumps and returned to Stornoway to unload them. At twelve next morning we sailed for Aultbea, arriving at 4 p.m. The weather was good and rough and the galley was flooded, so I shut the door and left it. I gave the ship's company steak for dinner that day and liver and bacon at night. They didn't like it much but I did it a different and special way and they really went for it. They were so fussy and used to carry on as though they were at the Ritz.

Overnight at Aultbea we tied up to the *Miner IV* and went to the Boom Base Pier to unload anchors, clumps, cables and wires. I went to the Aultbea Hotel for a drink with the lads and afterwards phoned Pauline. The sound here was excellent – beautifully clear – quite the opposite of what it was at Ullapool and Stornoway. I used to feel sorry for Pauline. She had to take these calls in a public phone box and hope it wasn't in use at the time I called.

Next day we changed a buoy and finished unloading from the Tolsta job. We also had to change a mushroom anchor for pick anchors in the Boom.

During our time in this area the lads caught a lot of fish, which I cooked for their tea. We had no electricity and so no fridge working. A night or two later the *Miner IV* came alongside to fix up emergency lighting. Meanwhile I had to write by oil lamp and candle.

Lighting had at last been restored and we were anchored at the small island in the middle of Loch Ewe. We had been changing the moorings on two Boom Defence ships that were 'in mothballs'. The *Miner IV* was laying wires under the sea at the entrance to the Loch. Some major exercises were due to take place in the near future.

The First Lieutenant was being authoritative again, saying that the stand-easy tea was being made a quarter of an hour too early and also that from then on the stokers should have their lunch at 12 a.m. instead of 11.30 a.m., as they always had had. The Leading Stoker had been put on a charge the previous day for having his lunch when he should have been working. The weather used to make life pretty rough sometimes, with broken cups, water and clothes everywhere.

The steward and I used to work together, helping one another. He generally served the two officers but sometimes I would take it on. One day, while cleaning the First Lieutenant's cabin, he found a draft for me, which meant that I was due to go back to Chatham, but a note was attached saying a letter was to follow. I believed that the Captain wanted me to stay.

By now we had almost finished work on the Boom moorings and might be sailing for Ullapool the following Monday. It was blowing up for rough weather and we might have to leave the pier that same night. The trouble with these piers was that they were made of wood and had to take a lot of battering. What with the bollard at Ullapool and the two stanchions here at Aultbea, we thought we would soon be banned from around these parts!

A few days later we were still working on the Boom, changing the pennants and anchors. We would be leaving some to the *Barbican*, which was to relieve us, as we had already done most of the work. The lads caught a lot of fish for dinner again, but they would be having steak pie for supper. They used to live well but never realised it. On the *Miner IV* they didn't have sufficient crew for a cook and had to make do with a Seaman to do the cooking.

We were anchored off the pier. The steward told me that a letter had arrived cancelling my draft. I hoped this was right. I was only an acting Leading Hand and if drafted, would lose £2 of my pay.

Five Frigates, a Carrier and two Tankers arrived. The following afternoon we went alongside the Carrier to take off airplane parts. As the first Frigate arrived, we were coming down the Loch towards the pier at the same time. She flashed 'Enter Harbour after me' so we turned and went round the other side of the island out of the way.

There was a lot of activity in Loch Ewe next morning. Three Norwegian Destroyers and two more Frigates came in. A major exercise was about to start but by the next morning we would be out of it. We were due to sail for Ullapool at 0800 hours, and would be coaling ship there, returning two or three days later.

First, however, we had another job to do on Loch Broom, near Ullapool, namely to recover an anchor which the frigate *Loch Alvie* had lost. At the mouth of the loch was a huge rock as big as a block of flats. The entrances on either side were quite narrow and for a large ship would have called for some tight manoeuvring. The rock itself must have been a bird sanctuary. It was covered in sea birds of all types and the racket they caused was quite deafening. Inside the Loch we found a huge expanse of calm, flat water. There was not a soul to be seen, but in the distance the ruins of a house could be made out. Clearly, someone had lived there many years before. The *Loch Alvie* had probably used those ruins to take a bearing.

We sent our diver down to look for the lost anchor and after some considerable time he reported back. When I asked him later what had taken him so long, he told me that the peat floating in the strong undertow was so thick that he could not see. He had had to walk backwards against the tow

Dressed as pirates to celebrate the Coronation, 1952. Our deep-sea diver on the left.

and eventually found the anchor by falling over it. He then managed to get a coupling on the cable and we hauled it aboard with our forrard steam winches. We then found another anchor attached to the cable of the *Loch Alvie* one, and so it went on and on! We had discovered a whole graveyard of cables and anchors, the latter being of all shapes and sizes, including a few from sailing ships. Some were so huge and heavy, and with such large cables, that it would have taken three men to lift a single link. We were there for hours and in the end we took what we could and left a marker buoy before carrying on to Rosyth.

The galley door was starboard side amidships and was a split door with separate top and bottom halves. The bottom one had a shelf to make it easier to use as a serving hatch for the messes. The cables were piled up, on both port and starboard sides, right to the level of this half door. To get into the galley, therefore, I was forced to scramble over the cables and climb in through the top half. To serve meals on trays to the messes was difficult for the messmen, who had to lie flat on the cables, taking their mess trays and passing them back astern or forrard. What a business!

One morning we had a good laugh. We were passing three Frigates going to the Boom Pier. As we were arriving, we were fetching black smoke. The Captain told the stokers to stop making smoke so they made more. They said it would make those Frigates realise that there were still coal burners left!

One day we were behind schedule. Three stokers had taken an Admiralty lorry and got as far as Gairloch before being stopped by the civilian police. I think it was more a bit of fun than anything, but anyway they were fined £10 apiece in court and now would have the Navy discipline to face with charges of being adrift, disgracing the Queen's uniform, being improperly dressed etc.

There was a general call to cheer up and we went ashore at Ullapool. Everyone – including myself – was upset with our new First Lieutenant and I had too much gin (which I normally don't like).

We had at last finished coaling and were due to return to Aultbea. At Captain's Rounds he commended me for the state of the galley. He said just the same thing as he said to the messes: 'a great improvement but there is still room for more'.

We arrived back at Aultbea with a gale blowing. A trawler was sheltering in the Loch and we bought about seven stone of fish from her for a hundred cigarettes. I soon made a hole in it when we had supper that night. We anchored out from the pier and no shore leave was allowed owing to the weather. This persisted even in the Loch itself, and no boat was lowered until several nights later. By this time it was October 15th and we would soon be leaving for a two-day trip to Rosyth.

At last the Captain decided to go alongside the pier, because though it had been blowing a 90-mile gale all day, it had now become much calmer. This, we believed, might be our last trip to Aultbea; there was also talk of spending a final weekend at Stornoway for a goodbye visit.

Next day we were working on the Boom until 6 p.m. and it was 6.30 before we got alongside the pier. As a result I missed Pauline's phone call. The divers were down to 110 feet and we all had our share at the pumps. However, they found the trouble and put it half right. They thought it would not take them more than another day to finish the job.

A few days later we were out on the Boom again, picking up buoys that were no longer wanted. From 4 p.m. onwards we had been anchored off the pier and were expecting to sail for Rosyth on 19th October, subject to being relieved by H.M.S. *Barbican*.

A night or two later I went to the Boom Defence Cinema. It was only an old Nissen hut but, at 7d, it was dear to get in. The lads had been fishing for Conger again and a stoker had caught one of 10 lbs. However, they never used to know how to kill them or skin them, which, however tough the skin, is an absolute necessity. Next day, a Friday, we sailed for Stornoway.

Yet another Force 9 gale was blowing, and we had a rough trip. But that evening we had a great run ashore with some fishermen we knew and there was a strong prospect of seven days' leave when we got to Rosyth. In the course of the day we had done some diving but had had to stop as both divers had found the pressure too much and had been unable to reach full depth.

We sailed for Rosyth about 6.30 p.m., hoping to arrive on the following Friday morning about 7 a.m., though we knew we would have to wait for the tide. Next night we passed Cape Wrath in good weather, and continued on through the Pentland Firth early in the morning, leaving Dundee off to starboard.

CHAPTER III

Rosyth

WE ARRIVED AT ROSYTH on 14th October, 1953. I was still not sure of whether leave would be granted but was hoping for a long weekend with an additional four days. The grounds for this were that we were working last Whitsun and also that we had only had one day's leave for the Coronation. I found that the routine for night leave in Rosyth was different from the one I had been used to. The Steward, the Signalman and I organised it between us. I was able to go ashore after supper and it was possible that I might get to Edinburgh on my Saturday night off.

After phoning Pauline, I went to the base pictures. Only fifteen of the ship's company were left on board, many of the hands having taken a long weekend. We would soon be de-coaling ship in preparation for going into drydock. All the plates were coming out on the port side due to the damage done by the pontoon the previous June.

We moved into the basin forrard of *Artifex*, ready to move into drydock. In the basin we found the Aircraft Carrier *Glory* opposite us, two Cruisers actually in drydock, and three Destroyers lying aft of us outside the Basin itself. With them were a few 'Bay' Class Frigates as well as Bar Boats, Tugs and other smaller ships.

After weekend leave, my train arrived back in Edinburgh one hour late and I had to see the Station Master to get our leave tickets properly endorsed. The ship was due to move into drydock the following day. That weekend I was on duty and found that the meat we were getting here – all mutton and veal – was so rough that it was impossible to roast.

One day the Padre came on board and was talking to us in the galley. At one point a Petty Officer put his head in and asked: 'What's the matter with the *** hot water?'

Two new stokers joined us, who had only been in the Navy for six months. The lads dressed them up in life jackets and told them to climb into one of the boats to look for the Fog Locker key. The Captain asked them what they were looking for and quickly hid his face. Next the lads told one of them to get a bucket of steam for the siren.

One day the First Lieutenant asked me whether I had done my foreign service. When I told him that I had not yet done it, he replied: 'You must be on top line for it.'

For a few days during our time at Rosyth, with only twelve on board, and with the Captain and First Lieutenant both ashore, I found myself Steward as well as Cook. But of course I had no worries about the Wardroom. Most of the hands too were on weekend leave and night leave.

Throughout *Barcarole* everyone was asking whether the ship was to undergo a major refit or merely a quick one. Eventually the news came through that it was going to take only a few weeks and that we would be out for trials before Christmas. A day or two later I had to take my Preliminary ETI (Educational Training Test).

By now, even though the ship had yet to enter drydock, she was already one great busy beehive and the hammering and rivetting were going full tilt. The noise was absolutely deafening – a proper madhouse!

The galley was being fitted with a new stainless steel sink and with three dockers working in it, my task was far from easy, to put it mildly. Then the First Lieutenant wanted to know why it wasn't so clean! That week the Steward was adrift getting back from leave, as he had been the week before, so as a result, he had a day's pay stopped and also seven days' leave. It was Pauline's birthday so I sent her some roses via the Naval Tailors.

At last, on 5th November, we moved into the drydock and they lost no time in taking off *Barcarole*'s mast. She looked a bit of a mess, being all colours but mostly red from the red lead. The water was still not all out of the dock and I concluded that they would leave that until the next day, when we would be lying flat on the bottom supported by beams on either side to keep us upright. Pauline had received the roses and I found that I could spend up to £30 a year done by allotment, that is by installments of so much a month from my pay.

One afternoon I had a good laugh. I thought of a good idea for cleaning the chimney. I stuck an 80 lb air-pressure hose up. It worked beautifully but covered the dockyard maties in soot. I got myself out of the way down in the mess, but the fire went a whole lot better!

The entire ship's company had to go to Edinburgh for an x-ray. This was probably a check to ensure that working on a coal-fired ship had not done any damage to our lungs. Fortunately in my case I was perfectly all right.

The galley was turned upside down, what with a reconditioned range being fitted and new washbasins being installed. Over and above the noise of chipping and hammering and the confusion of having cables all over the place, I had been using a windy hammer on the walls to get all the paint off and nearly deafened myself. For a short time we were forced to share a shore

Three shipmates on H.M.S. Barcarole.

galley with the Frigate *Tenacious*, which was highly inconvenient, with everyone getting in each other's way. Major repairs were carried out and the whole of the forrard peak was re-rivetted. In the messes, all the corkaseen was taken up and replaced.

A few nights later the Coxswain told me to stow away some of the galley gear by Thursday evening. When I protested at this, saying surely the weekend would be soon enough, he told me that it was hoped that we would all be away on Christmas leave by Friday night.

On Monday, 7th December 1953 we were afloat and out of drydock. We returned to our former berth forrard of the *Artifex*, which all of us knew as windy corner. We would be glad to be in operation again but meanwhile were getting ready for leave. They had taken our fresh water tank away to be de-corroded and for the time being we were having to use the bathroom on H.M.S. *Artifex*. I had a devil of a job with water!

Christmas leave was a wonderful break and I and Pauline had some great days together. When I came back, I found that a new stainless steel sink and preparing bench had been installed in the galley, though they had not yet been painted. All the lads kept asking about Pauline and wanting to know whether we had become engaged. I told them we still couldn't afford it.

We still did not know what our next station would be. There were rumours that we might be going back to Greenock or even to Aultbea.

Scapa Flow was also mentioned as a possibility. The Captain had been off for two days' duck shooting and I cooked the ducks he brought back for the Wardroom. The buzz was that he would be leaving in February and we all felt it was a pity that the First Lieutenant would not be going as well.

Easter leave was due to start on March 27th and painting ship had to be finished by the 17th of the month. There were no hands to spare for the galley and not enough time either, so I made a start myself and got quite a lot done.

I had a letter from Dad saying how pleased he had been to meet Pauline when I took her to see him on my Christmas leave. He was going to ask her to come again for a weekend. He had complained before, in one of his letters, that I didn't come to see him often enough. I was still painting the galley but it had turned bitterly cold and there was a very hard frost.

We put on a dinner party for the Wardroom. The menu was tomato soup, cod fillet, wild duck, roast potatoes, sprouts, orange salad, game chips, Christmas pudding and sauce. This was followed by coffee and fresh fruit. ('The Chef's efforts for the Wardroom will not go unrewarded'.)

We still had the old ship's wireless down in the mess and since the Captain and First Lieutenant were both ashore, we had been having Radio Luxembourg all over the ship. (The Captain didn't like Radio Luxembourg.) We were due to leave the Basin on Friday and go back to the coaling jetty to coal ship, after which we would be doing our compass and speed trials.

Once again they had given the galley the wrong coal – steaming coal instead of domestic, the devils! I couldn't get any heat out of it.

The Captain was due to take over a new Bar Boat in February – I believe she was in Singapore. A new Watch Bill had been made out since the rest had come back on Thursday. I happened to be on long weekend but I didn't think I would take it. If I signed on for another five years, I would get £100.

I cleaned the flues in the galley and got a mouthful of dust and a bleeding nose from it. I still hadn't finished painting; there was no green paint on board.

A few days later there was a hundred-mile gale blowing and we had to tie up at K3 Berth in the Basin. You could hardly walk against the wind and it looked as though we would have to stay where we were until it blew itself out.

Gales were still very strong round the coast. A relief came from Chatham, a Seaman who was only seventeen and a half. He lived in the Tower of London and his name was Johns. His father was a Beefeater and already he had been nicknamed 'Amberlin'. I moved out of the Petty Officers' mess into the forrard one, which is much warmer.

The next day we expected to be moving out of the Basin, which would make conditions much easier. We would be able to use our own toilets and ditch gash over the side without having to go ashore every time. We started coaling as soon as possible and there were also a number of minor jobs to be done and most of the superstructure still to be painted. The painting of the galley hadn't yet been completed either.

We were out of the Basin at last and took on a hundred tons of coal one afternoon. We were now tied up alongside the old timber jetty facing H.M.S. *Nigeria.* I went ashore to see a great western film called *Shane* and also went to see my tailor and managed to fit in a couple of lagers, arriving back on board by 10.30. The next night the Yeoman did supper for me but couldn't get any heat out of the range. In the end he gave it up as a bad job and gave the hands corned beef and eggs.

They brought me some different coal in the New Year but I found it was a darned sight worse than the first lot! I prepared a nice supper of roast veal, roast potatoes and cabbage. Next day there was a big lunch in the Wardroom. The Captain had been duck shooting again and wanted one for supper (he would!). He was doing Rounds on Saturday, which didn't please any of us much; there was so much cleaning up to do. It was a full-time job in itself. The day after that there was a Base Muster Check on all galley utensils: mess plates, knives, forks etc. In the afternoon I had to scrub my woodwork: the deckhead and bulkheads had to be washed down and in addition that same afternoon I had all my lightwork to do: brass scuttle, taps, copper lids etc., all to be given a nice shine. The amount of work you could find to do was surprising. Dad was expecting us that weekend but I had to tell him not to bother. The fact was, I couldn't afford it.

I hardly stopped all day getting ready for the next day's Rounds. As the seaman says, I 'scrubbed everything that moved and painted everything that didn't'. The ship was almost finished by now, though we still did not know what we would be doing – probably taking training classes out.

The new Captain came aboard one night and said to the Quartermaster: 'I am taking over the tub.' The First Lieutenant met him on the upper deck and said 'I am Commissioned Gunner French, Sir, your First Lieutenant.' The new Captain said 'Hiya' and walked straight past. He was First Lieutenant on the *Corregan*, the ship he had just come from, but had been Captain on one of these ships before and was said to be good when he had his own command.

The old Captain's Rounds passed off well with no faults or criticisms. He came into the galley and said it looked 100% better but that there was still plenty of time to put it in a liner's class.

The Captain wrote in his Night Rounds book that the ship was likely to be ready for service on the 1st February.

A few days after this we went up river to set the compass. We went under one arch of the Forth Bridge and back through the other one. Next day we coaled ship and hoped to get some proper domestic coal for the galley at last. We also went for a trial run.

A funny incident occurred with that Junior Seaman from the Tower. Bob offered him a sip of his rum and he downed it in one (poor Bob!). This lad offered Pauline and me a free day going round the Tower. On 16th of the month we had our Annual Inspection by the Captain of *Safeguard*. Before this we were due to go over to the South Arm to degalvanise. It had something to do with the ship being earthed properly and also with static electricity.

I developed a septic foot and was told by the Doctor in the Sick Bay on *Cockrane* to rest it after a penicillin injection. As a result they had to put a Seaman in the galley. When I finally got back on board, I found that the dinner was adrift to hell so I said I would go into the galley and do what I could. I did a mixed grill with pastry for sweet. That afternoon I was scrubbing out and the Seaman was cleaning out too. However, it didn't make a bit of difference because the cause of the dirt was all that rubbishy coal we had been given. The Coxswain came and blamed me for everything and I really told him the score. I was trembling with anger and the Seaman was actually holding my arm, thinking it was going to be 'fun and games'. I was also trying to clean the galley for the Captain's Rounds and was most annoyed, especially as I had volunteered in spite of my bad foot. The Coxswain put me on report so I went to see the First Lieutenant. He said he understood the situation in the galley and I could get the meals on time, so he put me on Captain's Report for failing to clean the funnels. He probably would have passed over it if I hadn't lost my temper with the Coxswain. I went on a second visit to the Doctor on *Cockrane* and he was quite pleased with the way my foot was clearing up but still wanted to keep me on penicillin and rest. When I arrived back on board, I went straight back to the galley and got things ready for Rounds at 11.30. Then it was off cap in front of the Captain. 'Leading Cook, you have exceptionally good papers and I would hate to be the first person to put anything on them.' The First Lieutenant had me on two charges: arguing with the Coxswain and failing to clean the flues and chimney. The Captain asked whether these were correct and I replied that the one relating to the flues was not. The flues got blown out once every two days and the funnel was not my responsibility. The ERA (Engine Room Artificer 5) backed me up and the outcome was: 'Case Dismissed'.

I wrote to Australia to enquire about emigration, but as I had five years reserve time to do, I couldn't go unless I joined their Navy.

My foot seemed almost better and the doctor was going to discharge me next day, but then it swelled right up again. I suppose it was a result of being on it all the time. I was still so busy in the galley.

The following day we were going out to survey a buoy and then we were alongside for our Annual Inspection. I found that we (Pauline and myself) got discussed down in the Mess. 'Hey, Chef, when are you getting married? How's Pauline?' Then the married men used to tell me what married life was like and then the finances of it would come into the conversation.

At the time we were alongside P Berth until we had been inspected by the Captain of *Safeguard*. I was now in Sick Bay on the *Cockrane* for a few days. One day the Doctor told me that I hadn't been resting my foot properly and I was still having penicillin jabs. Right old cruiser *Cockrane* was! Still, there was plenty of room and you could soak in a long bath. The food, however, was terrible and I could not eat supper. Lunch wasn't so bad but there was not enough of it. Pauline phoned me there, but with two others and the Sick Bay attendant nearby, it wasn't exactly private. Next day a Seaman came in after an accident which happened while his ship was alongside the North Wall. There was a buoy on the horns with wire and he stepped over this just as they were knocking the pin out. The wire caught him in the legs and shot him up into the air. He was shaken and bruised, but all he was bothered about was that his hat had gone over the side. His attitude was a bit like mine. I was patient enough having my foot treated and having jabs and poultices, but when they stopped my tot, I kicked up a hell of a row.

I had now been in Sick Bay for four days. The doctor said there was something in my foot which had to come out and I was to have more penicillin and poultices.

I returned on board to find everyone in a panic at the forthcoming inspection and dashing around. I kept telling them that it wasn't the Queen coming. A Supply Officer came to inspect the galley and the Captain phoned the Medical Officer to ask whether I could be released in view of the forthcoming major inspection. The Supply Officer was quite good. He asked me whether I had enough utensils and then asked the Coxswain how the cooking was. He replied that there were no complaints (so he had come round a bit). I decided to do the morning watch next day. There was so much to do in preparation for the inspection and I would have to wear full whites as well.

When the Base Captain came to inspect the galley, he asked me how I

Myself on Solebay.

managed the cooking with the coal being so bad. So I told him! The new Captain was due to arrive on board that Thursday.

By this time we were alongside the South Arm and would be moving to P Berth next day. The new Captain was due to come on board for lunch. The Steward and I would be giving a dinner for the two Captains and the First Lieutenant. Easter leave was due to start on the 29th March. One day the Steward overheard the Captain telling the First Lieutenant that it wouldn't be long before they lost both me and the Steward himself. (He had passed for Petty Officer.) Other cooks that had held this posting before me had gone after a year and our branch usually moved you around on these ships. *Barbican* had had three cooks in as many months, and all of them had asked for a draft. My galley had five officers in three days nosing around. One day I had a Medical Officer in there. Still, they didn't worry too much as long as the utensils were clean. Mine were well polished, so if that wasn't good enough – hard luck!

We had just finished cleaning up after the dinner party. The new Captain told the Steward that he had thoroughly enjoyed it and said how excellently cooked it was. He wished the Steward to mention this to me. I should think so, considering what they had: mushroom soup, fillet of plaice, mixed grill, pork, chopped liver and bacon, chipolatas, eggs, mushrooms, tomatoes, cauliflower, brussels sprouts, peas, asparagus in butter, fruit salad and cream. There were no tips – not even a pink gin or anything like that!

Before he left, the old Captain had a natter to us. 'When I joined the ship two years ago, it was nothing but an ill-disciplined rabble. Now this ship is the best I ever had. We all proved that at Aultbea. No job is too big and any job we are asked to do can be done in record time.' (Same old flannel!)

I was late again today, working in the galley and preparing a stew. Next day we were going out into the river, surveying buoys and picking up trots.

On 22nd February, 1954 my draft came through. I was to be drafted to RNB on relief. It had been a good crowd of lads on *Barcarole* and I would miss them. I saw the Captain and had a good chat. He would have liked to keep me on for another six months but said that he didn't like to mess about with the drafting board and that I was due for a spell of foreign service. (Little did he know that I was due to join H.M.S. *Ganges* at Shotley). So I would lose my acting rate and £2.10s pay per fortnight.

After a natter about the state the ship was in, the Captain granted all long weekends without requests. The First Lieutenant told me that afternoon that this was subject to the ship being alongside.

Due to the weather we remained in port, but I knew that if I didn't catch the 12.30 ferry to Port Edgar, then I couldn't catch the 1.15 bus to Edinburgh and would miss the 2 p.m. train to King's Cross.

We at last managed to go out into the river and check the moorings, a job which should have been done two days before. I served supper for the Captain and the First Lieutenant that night and the Captain called me 'Cooky'! He said he had enjoyed the meal and that he would miss my cooking. (Decent officer to talk to – just the opposite of the last one!) I told him I wouldn't be bothered if my relief didn't come. 'Tough luck', he replied. At times I hated the whole damn life in the Navy but it was the comradeship that kept you going. Everyone mucked in. So now it looked as though it was back to 'Get your hair cut', saluting, kit musters, night clothing, and being up at 6.15, though the last-named wouldn't make much difference to me. But I would only be on duty watch every four days, three weekends a month. I had a new paybook, so I would have to get a photograph for it.

When I arrived back from weekend leave, I found that my relief had come. He said he knew me but I couldn't remember him. He had been in for five years, so the lads would be all right. On the other hand he had no interest in the job and was finishing in a year's time. I was due to leave the ship on Thursday, so I would either join RNB that night or in the morning. My relief thought I had got the Carrier *Centaur*, going to Malta, Hong Kong and Japan (proper dreamer he was!). They had taken out 48 cooks from RNB in two weeks.

I left the ship at 1600 on my final day and would be in London at six or seven a.m. So that morning I strolled along to *Safeguard* and *Cockrane* to do my drafting routine, pay office, sick bay etc. At the bottom of the Night Order Book that night the Captain had put: 'I want to see the Leading Cook before he leaves the ship.' The lads had been passing a lot of rum my way that day. They knew it was the only drink I would have. I turned everything over to my relief, so I had finished with the galley. I was sorry to say it, but he simply wasn't interested. Already the state of the galley was shocking and things were not being done as I should have liked, but it would take time and I hoped he would pull his socks up. I had written my last letter from H.M.S. *Barcarole*, Boom Defence Vessel.

CHAPTER IV

H.M.S. *Ganges*

I BADE A CORDIAL FAREWELL to the Captain and crew of H.M.S. *Barcarole* and the Captain called 'Good luck' from the bridge as I left. I would miss my mates on her – a grand lot of lads. My immediate destination was the Royal Naval Base at Chatham, where I duly arrived at 10.30 a.m. That same morning I completed most of the joining routine, the medical, dental and other examinations. In the afternoon I had a kit muster and had to replace £3.2s-worth out of my pay. I was assigned to the Second Starboard Watch, which meant duty that weekend. After that I could get Watchkeeper's Leave at 1 a.m., so I would have time to get to London. There were rows of taxis waiting at RNB – the first time I knew that they were allowed in.

Having completed joining routine, I found myself installed on the second floor up of the *Collingwood*, where I stowed away all my bedding and kit. What a place that was to work in! I was assigned to the North Camp Vegetable Centre. The arrangement there was that all the vegetables were cleaned and prepared in one place and then sent to the galleys. I was put in charge of the Assistant Cooks and already I could foresee 'fun and games' with some of them. It was just my luck, I felt, to be duty weekend. It was said that all galleys were short of cooks and two of ours were leaving for postings in Malta.

We had just completed duty watch: 30 cwt of cabbage, one ton of carrots, and 49 bags of potatoes (done by machine, thank goodness) to clean and prepare! Duty weekend finished at 8.30 a.m., which gave me time to go and see Pauline at Lewisham.

I started preparing for my Educational Test. I found it hard going but was determined to stick at it.

A typical day under my new routine went somewhat as follows: by 8.30 a.m. we were all cleaning windows. At 11.30 we had our tots and lunch. At 12.30 we crashed out and at 3.30 got up and washed, and I went over for my tea. The NAAFI Club there was particularly good, I found.

The following Saturday Pauline came down to Chatham. I met her at the station at 12 a.m. Fortunately the inspection was not too long-winded; otherwise I would not have been able to make it. Next day I would be on duty watch any time before 7.30.

By this time I was getting into a steady routine: 6.30 up, washed and shaved, breakfast and work at 8.30, tot and lunch at 11,45, 1.45 work, 4.45 finish.

One day it was my turn to get up early (three of us). I managed to rise at 5.30 a.m., signed for the keys and opened up the Vegetable Centre, where I made a cup of tea and did some work.

Owing to shortage of pay (due to having to pay for my kit replacements), I would have to take casual work while on leave. John Hurst wanted me to try and go back with him on the *Centaur* but I said 'no thanks'! I wanted to write home to Dad; he would be wondering whether I was still in the Navy. I did write to him later, but only to tell him to emigrate to Australia so that I could change to the Australian Navy. He would go berserk when he read it!

We were all changed from the Vegetable Centre, and I got the job I wanted in the Bakery, where we did night work. We made the dough at 6 a.m., and baked it at 8.30 so as to have it finished by 1 a.m. There was a rest room nearby, so we would be mostly in there over the weekend. We had 1368 rolls to make next day and another 2000 for Monday. I had been working on the pastry machine and that afternoon I scrubbed the woodwork. We had finished before two o'clock.

That night I fell asleep on my way back from night leave from London and found myself in Gillingham. I lost my way and did not get back until 1 a.m. It was a good job I was on standby and finished at 3 p.m.

I was sent to another shore establishment, the Training Establishment for Cooks and Stewards, namely H.M.S. *Ceres*, near Wetherby. Seven days passed. I had a cabin to myself, complete with robe locker, carpet and chairs. It was a real home from home.

Next I arrived at my permanent assignation, H.M.S. *Ganges*, the training establishment for boys of between fifteen and seventeen located at Shotley, and at first I was feeling rather sorry for myself. The dining halls were all in one block with galleys above and below. They were only two years old. The main galley was huge but now and again they used to close half of it down and then open it again. All meals were served by us but most of the chefs were just out of training and a mad lot they were. There were 1860 boys to cook for and we were on a three-watch system. I didn't yet know which watch I would be in, but was hoping for a weekend at Whitsun. I could see Harwich and Felixstowe, and Ipswich was a forty-minute bus ride away. We had 20 days' seasonal leave, the same as the boys (and an improvement on the 13 I had been having), and also one week-end in three.

All the equipment was impressive and grand, all in stainless steel, and the washbowls had hand-driers nearby. The Parade Ground was gigantic. To get to the Regulating Office you had to cross the Quarterdeck and a row of studs marked the point at which you had to salute it. I resolved that one night it would be a good thing to take up all those studs.

One morning not long after I had arrived, I had to go to Cookery Office at 9 a.m. in my best suit to see the Captain. He asked me what my last ship was like and told me to pass my Educational Training Exam (ETI). The Duty Officer too told me I would be a fool not to.

During joining routine, it had been drummed into me that the boys must call me 'Sir' and that I must pull them up if they didn't. When they used to come for their meals (which were different from those of the ship's company) they had to show a card stating what mess they were in. On one occasion a Petty Officer Instructor stood by me and one boy had forgotten his card, so the P.O. stood him on one side. After half an hour the Instructor said:

'What did you say?'

'I forgot my card.'

'What did you say?'

'I forgot my card, SIR!'

But when they called me 'sir' I felt like saying 'shut up'! You could get into trouble even for talking to them. If they forgot to wear their hats in the open they were pulled up before they had gone ten yards or so. Then they would have to wear a tin hat for about three weeks, or so I was told. One night a class was being marched round in pyjamas. Someone had done something wrong and the whole class had had to suffer. The boys got five shillings a week. They were not allowed in their messes with their boots on. Working parties were constantly being sent to the galleys and got a lot of jobs such as scrubbing out coppers or washing up.

When I told one little chap to scrub out a gigantic copper, he said: 'Please Sir, I can't reach the bottom.' I told him to get right inside and there he was, squatting down and scrubbing away. There were one or two thieves among them, though.

I made a determined start on preparing for my Educational Test, but was finding it tough going and it was difficult to concentrate, what with the hours I was having to work and the places available for study.

My two great recreations at this time were swimming and going to the cinema and fortunately I had good opportunities to do both. It was just as well that I could swim. Any cooks who could not had their leave stopped until they had learnt how to.

Pauline was very generous in sending her marvellous cakes. She came down to Ipswich and we spent a nice day. She mentioned that a local boy from *Ganges* had 'gone over the wire' somewhere near her place and was being looked for. It did happen sometimes. I was still studying for that ETI.

One day I was up at 1.30 a.m. to prepare breakfast again. I didn't mind getting up with the lark, but didn't so much like the idea of getting the lark up! I cooked fried bread – 2000 slices! – and did a number of other jobs. I managed to get a swim in after a short spell of sleep. Five of the cooks were on Commander's Report for failing to turn up for swimming instruction – it looked like stoppage of leave for them.

I was up at 3.30 next morning and worked until 8 a.m. That afternoon I went to school again and from there went straight on into Ipswich to the Labour Exchange to see if there was a job going for Pauline there – but nothing doing at that stage. I was going by bus but an officer gave me a lift in his car, which I thought was very good of him.

One afternoon I was given a special job to do. Every weekend a number of boys from three divisions used to take a boat and go sailing and camp out. They took stores with them and I had to check these out: milk, sugar, tinned fruit, tinned peas, corned beef, cheese, jam, syrup, margarine, butter, potatoes, bread.

I was still working out our finances for myself and Pauline and wondering whether two could live as cheaply as one.

Jock, our Petty Officer Cook, gave me two boys to clean the top servery. Now a number of these boys were good workers, but this pair! I told one to get a broom. 'Please, sir, they have been put away. 'GET A BROOM – I DON'T CARE WHERE FROM!' I shouted at him. I certainly made that pair work – caught them talking once so gave them a mop apiece. They had only just finished mopping so I told them to do it all over again. I used to feel sorry for the boys and talk to them and I thought then that I could give them a job and leave them to it. But I found they would only half do it and get me a telling off. No more sympathy after that! Harry was told to go down to the Establishment Office, Married Quarters. It seemed one half of his garden wasn't being done, so they told him off about it.

I returned from weekend leave, in the course of which I took Pauline to hospital to have her wisdom teeth out. I had a preliminary exam a few days later and it was pay day as well.

Last Night Rounds were Security Rounds. An officer used check all the doors. I had keys to the 1 and 2 serveries, the ship's company servery and all stores, fridges, bread room, cookery office and then, of course, all windows. I was up at 3.30 and finished at 12 next day. I was also rum bosun.

The dreaded day came and I did the preliminary ETI and found it easier than I thought. The real one was to come later. I didn't get my swimming in that afternoon as I had an Admiral walking round. He came into the galley with the Captain and had a look round.

'Thank you again, Pauline,' I said to myself, 'for those lovely cakes.' In another one and a half hours I would be in school again. Most of the classes I used to take were on early morning watch and I couldn't concentrate to that extent. If I did the 'early early', I calculated that I could probably get out of the gate in time to catch a really early train.

Duty came round again and on a Saturday too. That was the one time in the week when the boys who went out came back late at night for a meal. That meant two chefs working all night. Some of us used to volunteer for the job in the hope of getting away early.

What a day it had been – all brain work and it had given me a headache! I was up at 3.30 and by 9 a.m. I was at school. Ron and I both passed the preliminary; we both got the same marks for arithmetic but he got less than I for English. Harry got more for his arithmetic but his English was poor.

What a lovely party we had one night! I got to Liverpool Street at 11.45 and waited until 12.30 for the train to come in. I got my head down and wasn't it good too – a first-class coach! I arrived at Ipswich at 4.20 and spent two more hours in the waiting room. It wasn't too bad but I knew I would be feeling it next day!

It was tailor's time again and I needed uniform shirts, collars and underwear. I heard that the Divisional Officer had caught Ron smoking and had told the Petty Officer Cook to run him in. Next I heard that he had got only one day's stoppage of leave – 'sixteens', we used to call it – which only meant two hours' extra work. A lot of cooks were putting in for drafts and getting them granted too. I guessed the Navy looked at it this way: if they were not happy, they were not working well. But the ones who didn't put in would probably be in *Ganges* for two years. I was asked to be best man at Ken's wedding and readily agreed.

One day 11 of us got picked up for stains on our jackets – the working ones. As a result, we had to go and see the Divisional Officer every morning for a week, and also have a kit muster on Saturday. He also brought out another order. If he heard anyone swearing at the boys or swearing at all, he would put them on a charge. Dad's birthday was coming round on August 18th and I thought I would buy him a really good snuff box. Pauline decided to buy a Vespa. It was a good idea though the deposit was £20.

The kit muster that had been arranged for Saturday was scrubbed; we only got told off. The Friday before I had to get all the food ready for the boys who were going camping over the weekend – banyan picnics, they used to call them.

We did have a kit muster after all, and the outcome was that I was a pair of boots down and some long stockings. I never used to wear them then but I still had to buy them, which would take £2 out of my pay and leave me short. The boys still often got shouted at a lot and I did my share; some of them were so solid! I later heard that Ron didn't pass his ETI though I did. The Chief Cook phoned to find out for us as they had not informed us. I told Pauline to put an entry in her diary that the *Ganges* Sunset Ceremony was going to be on TV on 24th August. The boys would be manning the mast with one of them, known as the button boy, standing upright on the very top.

I sent Pauline some money for my leave. We always used to have shows and bookings to arrange and coach outings, which we both enjoyed. Ron told me he had a job for me in a bakery and that his parents had asked me to stay for a week if I liked. Another cook had just got a draft chit to the Aircraft Carrier *Glory*, so that would mean another married quarters house standing empty.

A new order came out: the senior chef of our mess would get a shake at 3.30 and then shake the rest. Harry, who lived just outside the gate, was asked who was going to shake him and he replied: 'The wife – she is senior to me.' One day we were working from eight to four, trying to get the Cornish pasties done for the bag meals that the boys were to go on leave with.

We had a wonderful leave, visiting friends and relations, going to films, taking walks in the park and a river trip to Greenwich. We also visited Nottingham and Keyworth, a village nearby where Pauline was evacuated during the War. Ken's wedding went off well and I managed to buy them a nice present. We got back to *Ganges* on the 6th September.

A day or two later we were working from 8 a.m. to 3.30. By this time the boys were coming back and had until midnight as their deadline. I asked the Duty Officer about my rate and he said that due to my seniority, it should be through. He was going to get in touch with Royal Naval Base. I told him I was thinking of getting married and settling down here but he said they usually waited until your time was nearly finished – say 18 months – and then sent you on Foreign Service. I was trying to work out my finances as a Leading Hand, but found it a bit complicated. The one thing clear was that it was going to be a tight squeeze!

We had an Admiral coming round on Wednesday, so I guessed there would be a panic for cleaning up. I had family letters to catch up on, especially to my Gran, who would be getting the hump if I didn't write to her soon.

I still hadn't heard about my rate but comforted myself with the thought of all that back pay to come. My duties were going on nicely by this time and I had got into the routine – there was an altogether better feeling over work. I had a 'recommend' for my dinner one day too, and when I gave the P.O.'s banana trifle for their sweet at lunch, they had it for tea as well and were still coming back for more. I should explain that the Petty Officers' galley and mess were separate from the main galley and dining rooms.

We had Captain's Rounds again, but he used not to say much. On Wednesday the C.-in-C. of the Nore was coming and I was very much hoping that that was going to be the lot. We had certainly had to move ourselves!

Surprising how old these Admirals looked. This one had very deep, bright eyes, with masses of gold braid on his arms. We had to hide the deep fryer and frying pan as we had had no time to get them cleaned. I also had to clean my window and polish my bed and locker space, and of course we still had meals to prepare as usual.

I was all on my own cooking for about 40 and getting along very well. The President of the Mess asked me whether I wanted to stay over there, so of course I said 'yes' and he was going to see what he could do.

My duty watch that day was quite easy, but as I was taking the joint out of the oven, it rolled over and splashed hot dripping over my arm. Sometimes I used to have as many as thirty joints to handle and still didn't get burnt, but that one time I had to have an accident.

Mr Kettel told me one day that I would be rated in the very near future. Three of us were due, and I believe that for some unknown reason they had held us back. It probably had something to do with the inspection. At Captain's Rounds one morning, damned if that black cat of ours didn't walk straight in front of him. He went quite white and said: 'Get that out of the galley!' She was usually so good at staying right out of the way on these occasions.

One morning I was sent six boys to do the veg., washing up etc. One of the Petty Officers upset the frying pan all over the deck – grease everywhere. 'All right, Chef', he said, 'I will send some of my boys over. So then I had a dozen boys I had to find jobs for and I had them for an hour and a half. They were not allowed to touch the machinery at all or do any cooking, and you still had to watch them the whole time. If you didn't, they quickly got down to two speeds, dead slow and stop.

We found we had a thief in the Mess. I had my suspicions but couldn't prove anything. A chef had money stolen out of his belt one afternoon. Three of us were turned in and I was asleep. Chaps had been coming in and out all afternoon, or so they told me. Funny, though, how it always seemed to be amongst the younger chaps. It was just about the lowest trick going to thieve off a messmate.

A few days later pay day came round and I received about £20, so I realised I was out in my calculations. A Rear Admiral was coming next day for the ceremonial stirring of the Christmas pudding. All P.O. cooks and wives were coming too, and probably we would have a galley full of gold braid. It was a good job I was in my galley out of the way, although he would have a look in at us beforehand.

Some days after this I heard that a bed had become spare in the P.O.s' Mess due to a chap buying himself out of the Navy. So I asked whether I could move in and was told that it would be a good idea in view of the fact that I was now permanent. The Leading Chef, who had his leg in plaster, would be staying there too and when he was taken off light duties, we would work watch and watch about. That same afternoon I got two boys to bring over my kit and bedding. So when I came back from leave, my new address would be: P.O.s' Mess, or 61 Mess. My mail would come directly there. It was not so far to get to work either. No Night Rounds either, although we had Captain's Rounds one morning. I stood them in the galley. He used not to say anything but I knew where he would look.

I decided to see our Divisional Officer to find out whether I was to get my issue before leave. I had just realised that when I got back, I would be in charge of all cooking (chefs and P.O.'s), so I guessed there would be plenty to do. I still didn't know anything about the Christmas puddings and cakes. I should, no doubt, have a turkey and would have to get the menus printed. I had compliments for my soup and pastry.

I spent my leave at Market Deeping, where there was widespread flooding and all the fields were waterlogged. Pauline and I spent 17 of the 22 days together and had a marvellous time.

When I got back from leave, I was greeted with cheers and shouts. I had my lunch and a tot and tried to see Mr Kettel, but he wasn't to be found. When I did see him, he had a weeks' pay for me, £4. I then realised just how busy I was going to be. The GMG was closing down and I would be having Harry, Starky and one other over in my galley. I was not working in a Watch, so I would have no duties until all the boys were back from leave. I was in charge of everything but only had to supervise. I had also to make sure that the security fire party had checked the GMG after the workmen had finished and all sorts of other jobs.

The day came when they had just about cleaned out the *Ganges*. I had only about 16 P.O.'s on board until Thursday, when we would be cooking for the entire ship's company of over 60 (including six officers).

One afternoon a few days later I drew and cleaned two turkeys, with Buck's help, and we put them back in the fridge. I still had no idea how many there would be for Christmas. There would only be about 20 on board and not many wives. I hoped to get the puddings and cakes over next day and we would have to put them in a safe place. I missed my tot one day so the next I had a neat one.

The festivities reminded me of *Barcarole* days. On Christmas eve I went ashore with the lads and we had a good singsong in Ipswich. The cooking went very well and everyone thoroughly enjoyed themselves. The menu included turkeys, ham, pork etc. There were problems in the distribution as we had three different places to deliver to and had to use food containers. The numbers were changed too. Only two of the wives came in the end. My tall hat was just the job, and with full whites I looked very smart and clean. The victualling P.O. told me that I was recommended for the previous day's turn out, though naturally I didn't take all the credit. After leave, he said, I could go through for my P.O.'s rate. That would mean six weeks in Chatham. It could have spelt danger, though, as it might have shaken up the drafting people. I had 'recommends' all round and the P.O.'s gave me a cigar and also a good drop. I was being very kind to the Ship's Company Regulating P.O. in particular, and hoped to be able to fiddle a weekend before long – perhaps New Year's Eve.

Mr Wallis came in today. 'I hear that you did very well over Christmas, Chef. Have you gone through for P.O. yet?' I told him I hadn't. 'You had better, then,' he said.

The P.O.'s had been directing the boys on the buses back from leave, so I cooked them egg, bacon and chips and they were happy enough. There was a possible house in married quarters: full three bedrooms, furnished and all gear for 35 shillings a week. But by now Pauline and I were talking about the New Zealand Navy.

I had to collect special food containers for all the meals to be taken to various parts of the establishment. Since I was on duty, I told the other cook he could go ashore as he had just got married and his wife was in Ipswich. He went but came back dead drunk so I had that to sort out. I would have seven cooks coming over when the main galley closed the following day and would have to organise watches. Two cooks were due to go on leave on the Monday and I would be going myself on the Tuesday, so that would leave me with a possible four. Some time in the next three weeks I would be going on draft. I had a sheet to work out organising the Security Patrol as well and a big sheet of orders working out who we were to cook for and why. Our three kittens had grown and had lovely markings.

Pauline and I had finally rejected the idea of the New Zealand Navy. When we had Captain's Rounds one morning, he was quite pleased. I was gradually getting him trained!

On Saturday morning about a dozen boys came over to work and a parcel arrived from Pauline. I undid it upside down by mistake and the lid came off. There was paper all over the place but the box was empty – no cake and no chocolates. 'What's wrong, Chef?' I was asked, 'No waste paper baskets where she works?' 'Sends her rubbish to the one she loves,' etc. It would have been all right if I had been on my own in the galley but it was full of P.O.'s and boys. I said: 'It's all right, she's mad. I get one of these every week.'

The phone that Pauline used to get through to me on was on its own on a bend in the stairs to the P.O.s' messes – something like a kiosk made of wood. I used to sleep in the same room where I wrote my letters. There were only five of us in there. At the bottom of the stairs was a P.O.s' Watchkeepers' Mess for Quartermasters and P.O. Stokers. The galley was at the bottom of the stairs, so I had only 20 steps through the galley to the dining room. Then came the entrance hall, beer bar, billiard room, lounge, TV room and a radio in each mess. The cinema was held in the gym. Fred, the Leading Chef who used to be down here, often used to drop in. He was down in the Sick Bay galley because 200 of the boys were down with flu. He also asked whether I wanted a draft but I said 'No thank you'.

While I was having my bath one night, two messmen called out 'Shore telephone call for you!' I rushed out, dressing myself as I went, only to meet them both laughing their heads off!

Some days later it was Quarterly Settlement and my pay came to £26 – more than I had expected. I had been wondering how much to put in the bank.

I had a little trouble with my beef that day – nine lbs of beef and three lbs of fat. I returned the fat and did the butcher moan! I referred him to Mr Wallis and in the end he gave me three lbs of beef for the fat.

Minnie, our cat, was an exceptionally good mother. One night we found a wild kitten and managed to get it into the galley but it was scared and crying. Minnie went up to it, washed it all over and we gave them both some milk. Now they have accepted one another and bonded together.

I asked Mr Kettel if I could go through for my P.O.'s rate and he said 'Yes, but first I will have to check whether you still have to do a year as Leading Cook.' I phoned him again soon afterwards and he had got through to Chatham. They had all they wanted going through for P.O.'s, many of whom had done more time than I. So he said that if there was a vacancy, I could go. However I didn't think he wanted me to go. Duty had been going very well and I was certainly getting popular with the P.O.'s. They remarked on the cleanliness of the galley and the tasty meals, so on the work side life here was very smooth and everyone quite happy. Still, I could get adapted to any galley and routine and usually got along very well if left alone. The work used to get done so much better. Easter leave was due to begin on the 7th April, '55, and being chefs, we would be able to go a few days earlier.

Mac and I got on well over the weekend. On Sunday I got up early and gave one of the P.O.'s a shake – Mac's job really but it gave him an extra lie-in. Poor old Newstead had been drafted and had had to move out of his married quarter. The trouble was he had a wife and two children and though he had been on the housing list for about 18 months, he still had nowhere to go. Also he had got his own furniture. He was referred to the Welfare Officer, a retired Major who lived in Ipswich. He was promised that he would not be turned out until he had found somewhere else to live.

I had a lovely hot bath one afternoon and it certainly developed into a skylark. For a start one of the messmen turned the water off and then opened all the windows and locked the door. So I climbed through the window and went round.

We had no hot water in the block for a time. The ERAs had been working on the Clarifier all day and I had to get hot water for my bath from the galley. I carried it all from the copper, filled the bath, came up for soap, towel and clean shirt, and then found someone had pulled the plug! The hot water would be back on again the next day.

We had the social and dance and were very busy making jellies and sandwiches, and that was on top of my ordinary work. It all went very well and the Captain and Commander came in for an hour. Everyone enjoyed themselves. I turned in just after 1 a.m. I had the job of looking after the band, who were quite happy as they had been given a crate of beer.

I travelled back from leave in a thoroughly gloomy mood. Walking past the serving window, I got a spoon thrown at me and boos and all sorts. 'Get married?' I was asked, and then 'Why not?' I saw the President of the Mess that afternoon. 'Thank God you're back.' The cook who had been sent over in my place had been changed to Leading Cook, but the President nearly put him in the rattle. He told Mr Kettel off for sending me on advanced leave and played merry hell with everyone involved. He said: 'The things I have said about you, you should get your Chief's rate'. The food had been shocking and the complaints had been piling up.

By this time I had two inexperienced cooks left here and in view of the trouble there had been while I had been on leave, I couldn't see them doing a duty on their own. I had that damn Security Patrol to organise again too. The painters were in. They were doing the Mess above and would be in here either the following day or the day after that. It had been a busy duty for me and I had been running around organising hot food containers and safari

4Ck(S) Parker

~~Ch.~~ Post Room CMB

Establishment Office,
H.M.S. Ganges.

7th December, 1954.

Establishment Officers
Temp. Memo. No. 134

Security Patrols Duty List.

DATE	WATCH	MIDDLE WATCH ROUNDS	FIRST WATCH ROUNDS.
Tuesday 14th December	Port	Yeo Sig. Hayles.	L/Tel Hand
Wednesday 15th December	Starb.	Shipt. Smoker	L/Stwd Laurenson.
Thursday 16th December	Port	Ch.Wtr. Curzon	L/Wtr Dunkley
Friday 17th December	Starb.	Shipt. Gridley	L/Ck (S) Parker
Saturday 18th December	Port	Shipt. Huxtable	S.P.O(V) Sheppard
Sunday 19th December	Starb.	Shipt. Mayhew	L/Ck (O) McKenzie.
Monday 20th December	Port	Yeo Sig. Hayles	L/Tel Hand
Tuesday 21st December	Starb.	Shipt. Smoker	L/Stwd Laurenson
Wednesday 22nd December	Port	ChWtr. Curzon	L/Wtr Dunkley
Thursday 23rd December	Starb.	Shipt Gridley	L/Ck(S) Parker
Friday 24th December	Port	Shipt. Huxtable	S.P.O(V) Sheppard
Saturday 25th December	Starb.	Shipt. Mayhew	L/Ck(O) McKenzie.
Sunday 26th December	Port	Shipt. Smoker	L/Stw. Laurenson
Monday 27th December	Starb.	Ch.Wtr. Curzon	L/Wtr. Dunkley
Tuesday 28th December	Port	Shipt. Gridley	L/Ck(S) Parker
Wednesday 29th December	Starb.	P.O.Wtr. Quance	P.O.Std. Cooper
Thursday 30th December	Port	Jnr. Gray	S.P.O(V) Sheppard
Friday 31st December	Starb.	C/Jnr.Gant	Jnr 4 Scowan
Saturday 1st January	Port	Shipt Bowmer	Ld.Ck(O) McKenzie
Sunday 2nd January	Starb.	Ch.Wt. Curzon	L/Wtr. Dunkley
Monday 3rd January	Port	Shipt. Wood	L/Ck(S) Parker
Tuesday 4th January	Starb.	NORMAL ROUTINE	

ATTENTION IS DRAWN TO COMMANDERS LEAVE ORDERS RE SECURITY PATROLS.
DUTIES COMMENCE AT NOON FOR 24 HOURS PERIOD.
SECURITY PATROL BOOK IS KEPT AT THE MAIN GATE. SHOULD ANYONE FALL SICK ETC. THE RATING WHO IS LONGEST STAND OFF WILL CARRY OUT THIS DUTY AND ROOSTER.AMENDED AS NECESSARY.ANY QUERIES TO REGULATING OFFICE.

(Sgd) R. E. Butt.

Lieutenant Commander R.N.
Establishment Officer.

Patrols Duty List, H.M.S. Ganges, *7th December, 1954.*

jars. These latter were gallon thermos flasks costing £6 each. All the P.O. Instructors had to be up at 3 a.m. to get the boys up, as they had to be paid, and the boys who had a long distance to travel would have to be away at 4 a.m. Many of the P.O.'s would be going with them. So I had to be up at 2.30 a.m. to cook breakfast for the P.O.'s.

What a state the galley was in! A damned safari jar had been smashed and everything was in chaos. The cook was only young and inexperienced so there was no use in getting in a state with him. What the food had been like I didn't know. Numbers were down to 44 by this time. Our mess was being painted. I hoped to be back up there next day and already it was beginning to look smart – green and cream. I hoped it would be all right for Captain's Rounds the following day.

A few days later I heard that I had a draft to H.M.S. *Defender*, Daring Class, and that she would be sailing for the Med. in June – nine months there and nine months in the Home Fleet. I was due to go on draft from *Ganges* on 2nd June.

Minnie brought all the kittens down to the galley again one afternoon, so I just put them in a box and took them all back up again. But Minnie, the offender, just called them down and the way they got down the steps – slide, slither and fall – made me laugh.

The Captain was in London, which meant that we wouldn't be paid until the following Thursday as he was the only one with authority to issue enough money for 60-odd.

Ten Sea Cadets came in from Chatham on a Frigate, and I had them in for supper and gave them breakfast next day. I had to move to the chief galley, which I didn't like so much as my own, but I wouldn't be able to get back to my own for a few days. Practically all the Ship's Company were back now, and all the boys were due back the following day – the day I moved back into my own galley.

I was up at four the morning the boys came back and had to chase the others and work damned hard myself, but we got the job done. When I got detailed for draft, I had to report to the Regulating Office. Then I had to go through the whole drafting routine, which involved having a card and getting it stamped at every office: the Pay Office, the Captain's Office, Establishment Office, DSO Clothing Office, Loan Clothing Office, Cooking Office, Sick Bay, Dental, C. of E. Chaplain and one or two others as well. It took the whole of the forenoon and the routine in Chatham was much the same.

About 8.30 in the evening, after a very hard day's work, I was piped to report to the Officer of the Watch. When I reported he told me that two boats, with 27 Boys, had got stuck in the mud, so that meant extra work making sandwiches, tea and so on. A lorry took it to them so I locked up again at 9.45 p.m. Then when I took the keys back, the Officer of the Watch said:

'There's a boat on its way back from somewhere else and you may be required again'! I decided that if I did get called out again, I would just stop up, as I had to be in the galley at 1.30 in any case.

Those boats that used to go off sailing at the weekends sounded like good fun, I imagined. I finished at 9 p.m. and did not have to turn out again after those boys after all.

Next day I was not on Divisions, which was a help. I had managed to dodge that for the last time. One day one of the lads asked a boy what his mother thought of him joining the Navy. He said he didn't have a mother – only a step-mother, and then burst into tears.

The Chief Cook said he would 'phone Chatham on Friday morning to ask whether I was still detailed for the *Defender*. I then heard that it was right, and that I had to go for a 'Pulheem', i.e. a medical examination. The word stands for 'Physical, Urine, Legs, Height, Eyes, Ears'. You had one every year if the powers that be were fortunate enough to catch you.

The information here was taken from the last letter I wrote from *Ganges* until 21st June. I wrote it while waiting for the pipe, 'Watchkeepers' Libertymen Fall In'. Pauline's mother was at Liphook, staying with a relation during a train strike. On 7th I went to the Registry Office and sent a telegram to Dad.

On 9th June 1955 I went again to the Registry Office at Harrow and we got married. Ursula, Pauline's Dad and Beeby were present. We stayed the night at the Sun Hotel, Chatham and phoned everybody on 10th. I went back to the Barracks on 11th only to find that I was on duty weekend. So I paid a sub to do it for me and stayed on at the NAAFI Club, followed by a dash to Mrs North's on 13th. I left early and joined the *Defender* at Chatham.

CHAPTER V

H.M.S. *Defender*

IT WAS THE LAST DAY of May 1955 and I had already left the *Ganges*. There had just been time for a final quick dash up to London – hitchhiking there and back – to see Pauline, write to Dad and see a few friends, and then I left by lorry for the Royal Naval Base to complete joining routine. I started off very early on the morning of June 13th, catching the trock boat to Sheerness, and was on board my new ship by 8.30. Straightway I found myself on Duty Watch with another cook. In the course of the day I had to Close Up on my Action Station. I was on Starboard STAAG – in other words, a Stabilised Automatic Anti-Aircraft Gun. I was No. 1 in the team, which meant that it was my job to supply the ammunition. 'Pass the ammo. – that's me', I said to myself. But thank goodness it was only for one day. The following day we were due to sail to Portland at 11 a.m. and arrived about 7 p.m. However, we didn't go in but anchored all night off Weymouth and left for Gibraltar at 7 a.m. By that night we had reached the Bay of Biscay. We we were all ready for Captain's Rounds but he didn't take them. In the course of the afternoon we passed Guernsey and I was able to get a letter off by airmail to Pauline. We were still in two Watches in the galley. The Divisional Officer thought it was a good idea to stay as we were. Someone would have to bake the bread but the time for this had not yet come. I had already made contact with the Radio Operator, whose name was Pete. He came back 29 minutes late from his weekend and got two days' leave of pay stopped – all because he had failed to get the Station Master's signature to say that the train was late.

Through the Bay of Biscay it was already getting notably warmer and we had no trouble from the great ocean outside. I heard that the Chef was going to start baking the next night but since I was already due to be up early in the morning, he decided to get another chef to do it. He didn't want to make me work all night. A few days later we changed into shorts and already I was looking forward to a spot of sunbathing on X Gun Deck. We were due to start exercises as well, even though it was confirmed that the *Delight* had engine trouble and that we would be on our own all the way to Malta.

We left Sheerness at 11 a.m. and when turning up the Channel, fired a

H.M.S. Defender, *Commissioning at Chatham.*

salute. We passed the White Cliffs about an hour later and were due to arrive in Gibraltar on the 29th, leaving there for Malta (if all went according to plan) on 1st July. Ten Marines joined us to take passage to Gibraltar. They were part of a band due to join *Jamaica*. We had a number of exercises on passage: Evening Quarters, Fall In for Emergency Stations etc. All kinds of 'emergencies' were practised, such as 'fire' or 'man overboard'.

The Chief Cook was still working two Watches and as soon as he stopped, he put me on day work. This meant that I would be baking. I had to wear clean whites every day but the fact that all the cooking was electric made it far easier to keep clean. I foresaw that when we got to Gibraltar, I would have to buy new white tropical shirts and trousers as well as stockings and badges. We were due for a refit when we got there. It had been planned that H.M.S. *Delight* would be joining us some time in October but then news came that she had had generator trouble and would be delayed. I hoped that working in the galley in the Med. would mean extra money for me, as well as separation money. By this time I was getting used to the routine – so different from that on *Ganges*. Pipe down was at 9.30 and we were up at 7 a.m. To me it seemed a funny routine but apparently it had always been the same. I enjoyed being at sea again,

H.M.S. Defender *entering Grand Harbour, Malta.*

especially as the Channel was exceptionally calm and there were spectacularly beautiful sunsets.

By the time we were passing the coast of Portugal, it was becoming really hot and we were wearing shorts and sandals. I was going to have an afternoon on X Gun Deck but discovered that it was being fixed, so I had to wait a few days longer. By this time I was settling in well, although of course it was a pretty tight ship. It was quite different from the *Barcarole*. I was detailed for a landing party and thought I would look pretty smart with a sten gun. Before long I began to get overseas allowance of 3/- a day, which would put my money up by £5 a fortnight.

On the day when I was fixed up with landing gear, it took me all the forenoon to go through the formalities. I had to draw webbing, rucksack and water bottle, entrenching tool and revolver. As part of our exercise we fired the 'Squids' and they went from the quarter-deck over the bridge and superstructure to hit the water in front of us, at which point the ship would perform a sharp turn. The explosion was far bigger than that of a depth charge, and had a much louder bang. We passed three Darings going home; they had finished their nine months in Malta.

The next day we were due to get into Gibraltar where all the mail would be waiting for us. I had spent about half the day sunbathing. Some of the lads were already red raw. It could be extremely painful and anyone who got too sunburned – to the point of being unable to work – got put on the First

Lieutenant's Report. I expected to have more free time now that I was on day work. The Chief wanted the chefs to get used to the routine before changing from two to three Watches.

Sure enough, when we got into Gibraltar, we found a bumper mail waiting for us. I found that the Chief Cook was one of the best, but he was understandably a little dubious about putting the chefs on their own. Three of them had never been to sea before, so he decided to put them all on day work alternatively. I was to start on Saturday and the following week another cook was to take over. At 9 a.m. we entered the harbour and fired a salute to the C.-in-C., Gibraltar. For some reason which I couldn't fathom, we did not go alongside but secured to a buoy outside the Destroyer pens. Quite a few of the lads went ashore and I asked them to get some postcards. I remembered I had been here in '51 and the things I bought then! I was already making arrangements for Pauline to come out to Malta in October for a holiday.

I found *Defender* quite a happy ship, although, at this stage anyhow, discipline was somewhat strict. I felt that it would be bound to slacken off before long. I had several reasons for deciding not to go ashore. First, I had no money and would not be getting any for two days, second, I was on duty the following day, and third, on the day I was off duty, we were due to sail, fourth, I doubted whether we would be in Gibraltar again until we were coming home. In my latest letter to Pauline I told her not to forget to apply for a passport and also flight papers, which had to be stamped by our Captain (whose name happened to be Hardie – different spelling from that of the famous Hardy of Nelson's day). Only if they were stamped by Captain Hardie, could she obtain a reduction in her air fare.

From Gibraltar we slipped away at 7 a.m. into the blue Mediterranean, which was as calm as a duckpond. All day we had shoals of dolphins around us. I spent the afternoon on the upper deck and it was so hot that everyone was perspiring under a fierce sun. There were no Rounds, which was a relief. The Chief changed his mind again and decided to put me on day work in Malta after all. Having done it all before, I didn't mind which I did.

We spent the first day or two doing a lot of manoeuvring. We finished early in the galley the first evening for a change, and as can be imagined, in the sort of weather we were having it was very hot working there. We were given an issue of lemon crystals daily, and used to mix them with sugar and iced water to make lemonade. I drank pints of the stuff, which was commonly known as 'limers'. Hence the Americans' name for us, 'Limeys'.

From then onwards I was on day work, which made things a little better. One afternoon one of the young cooks fell asleep on the Upper Deck and

Three of us. On the right is the Leading Seaman who lost the watch his wife had given him.

got himself badly sunburnt. The following morning, when he went into the galley, he almost flaked out with the heat and was given 24 hours 'excused duties'. We were all taking salt tablets. I had never drunk so much water in my life and we were told that the seven of us had got through enough lemon crystals for 210 men in under three days! The quality of food on a ship must have been thirty percent better than in shore establishments, especially with regard to meat and vegetables. Of course everyone was allowed a little more too.

I took an early opportunity to see the Supply Officer and he asked about Pauline and how she was getting along at home. I mentioned that we were hoping to get her out to Malta for a holiday. He said it might be possible to get some leave in October if she came out then, but that it was up to the Captain. He also told me that the return flight to Malta cost £38, not £32 as we had supposed.

The next day we arrived at Malta. We had Maltese officers' cooks on board and asked them how the musical boxes were in Malta. They said that we should wait until we reached Naples; they were cheaper there.

One day one of the Leading Seamen was in the whaler, retrieving a dummy Squid from the sea. Just as they were hauling it up into the boat, a rope took his watch off his wrist and it was lost. His wife had given it to him and had had it inscribed on the back – a sad loss.

We arrived in Malta on 4th July and tied up between two buoys in Grand Harbour, Valetta. A large amount of mail was waiting for us, which we eagerly devoured. I took the opportunity of getting myself measured for a white suit and was hoping it would soon be ready. Yet I only needed the darn thing for Divisions. One morning, soon after we arrived, the C.-in-C., Mediterranean came aboard and told our Captain that we would soon be off to Venice for the film festival and then on to Yugoslavia.

One night I did duty in the galley for another cook, Mick by name, who had a boil on his stomach and had to have it lanced. For the next ten days we were painting ship and were then due to go to sea for a fortnight. This meant that we would be spending only ten days a month actually in harbour in Malta. By this time the temperature had risen to 110 degrees and I had developed a real tan.

One night there was a medical emergency on board a passenger ship and we had to rush a doctor to her. However, when we arrived, we found that a Cruiser had beaten us to it.

According to the officers' chefs it took them six hours to fly them to England, so I concluded that it would take Pauline much the same to get to Malta. 'Phoning home to England cost 15/6 a minute, so I felt that from Malta it would be even more expensive, and I simply couldn't afford it.

Soon we were at sea again. Baking the bread was the job of the day cook. We used to start in the galley at 8 a.m. and work until 11 a.m. Then we would start again at 6 p.m. and make the doughs, which would be baked most of the night. All the time we were at sea rumours were constantly flying round the ship. One was about our programme for the next few months. It was believed that we would be in Malta for 14 days, then at sea for the next 10, then back for a week. After that we would be at sea again for a week, then back again for another three days in harbour before going on a cruise to Venice, Yugoslavia, Toronto and taking part in NATO exercises. We would be coming back to Malta about the middle of October and in drydock there up to three days before Christmas. In February we would be off again on a cruise to the south of France and taking part in combined Mediterranean and Home Fleet exercises. Finally we would be returning home in March. So the rumour ran, but as it transpired, it did not turn out like that at all. Those rumours!

I soon discovered that contrary to what I had thought, we would not be getting any extra money for working in the galley. This applied only to the Far Eastern Station. So all I would be getting extra was the usual 3/6 a day, which would put my pay up to £4.10s or £5 a week. We had 22 messes and

A short break from the galley.

a loudspeaker in each. The Captain had returned to active service after 10 years of civilian life. In preparation for Pauline's visit, I bought a number of photo albums from the P.O. SBA. They cost only £5 and he generously said I could pay him when I liked.

To relieve ourselves from the fierce heat, about fourteen of us went bathing in a place opposite to the ship, only to be stopped and told that members of our crew were not allowed to bathe in that particular place. Every other ship – yes, but ours had to be different. On every other ship the crews used to work stripped to the waist; only on ours did we have to wear shirts in the afternoon, both on the Upper Deck and below as well. One day a Naval Chaplain came to visit us and we had a moan to him about it. 'Leave it to me,' he said, and from then on we didn't wear shirts. The doctor had something to do with it too. He mentioned that a number of ratings were getting sweat rash.

Another day I had a damned landing to take part in – as if I did not have enough on my plate already. I was off duty next day as the Chief sent another cook down aft to do the one I would normally have been doing. Next day I was on again and this would go on until Mick was well enough to take over once more. Then it would be back to the forrard galley once more, but we had only a salmon salad to do for supper.

In full whites.

After completion of painting ship, we left harbour for ten days at sea, mostly with gunnery trials. After that, we believed, we would be on our own again for a week and then out with the Americans. When we returned from that we would be going on a cruise.

One day we went swimming in Vhecastley. To get there we took a Maltese type of boat known as a dghaisa – pronounced 'dyso' It was rowed by a man standing at the stern, something like a gondola but less ornate. This one had been contracted out to the ship. Vhecastley was the Fleet bathing place, situated at the rear entrance to Grand Harbour. We used to wear white shirts and shorts, long stockings and black shoes to go ashore. We had to be back by 7 p.m. to change into long blue trousers and tropical shirts with open necks. Alternatively we could go ashore in full whites. Our various rigs were known by numbers. Thus No. One was the tailor-made rig which I wore at my wedding. No. Two was the suit that I left with Pauline. No. Three was a blue serge suit, No. Six was whites with medals, No. Seven the same without medals. No. Eight was working dress, No. Ten blue shirts, blue shorts, stockings and sandals.

When it was too late to go bathing, I used to take a shower. At this time we were having plenty of cold meat and salads, and all in all doing pretty well. Then one day I had to go down to join the landing party and we were due to fall in at 3.15 p.m. wearing No. Eights. That meant wearing boots, which was not very good news for me – I hadn't got any! So I called over to another chap who took size tens. That solved one problem but unfortunately his boots had no laces. I called out again and this time got fixed up with laces, but it cost me a wet of my tot.

We had rigged up a water fountain on the mess deck and the water was refrigerated and ice-cold as it came out. Just as well too, with temperatures still in excess of 100 degrees.

The next thing that happened was that we became Second Flagship of the Second Cruiser Squadron in the Home Fleet. In the Home Fleet we were classed as a Daring, but out here as a Cruiser. We were like the the blooming Marines – neither Army nor Navy! On Sundays the ship was open to visitors and nearly everyone in the mess had decided to have an afternoon in Sliema. It was only a sixpenny bus ride to the other side. The attraction was that there was a lagoon there as well as a beach, so we took our 'big eats'. Naturally, therefore, they would not be going without me! One could have a lot of fun on 'banyans' of this sort, but we had to be back by six p.m.

When the First Lieutenant did his Rounds, he caught a lot of ratings without shirts on and put them in the rattle. He said he would be coming round again to make sure that they had got them on. The actual orders were that we could go without shirts from 12.30 to 6.30.

One day I had to do duty because one of the cooks was too inexperienced to be trusted on his own and needed to be helped out. There were pictures that night on X Deck and we saw a Ginger Rogers film. H.M.S. *Delight* arrived and I discovered that one of the cooks on her was a Leading Cook with whom I used to hitchhike from Chatham. He came on board to look me up and we decided to have a shore run that night, probably to have a drink and go to the pictures. The *Eagle*, which was lying astern of us, was due to go home for repairs which could not be carried out in Malta. She was a funny looking Carrier. I found that I was still getting cracks from my shipmates about the length of Pauline's letters: 'another book', 'daily manuscript', 'What the hell does she find to write about?'

After a time the routine in the galleys was changed. and we went into three Watches, two in a Watch. We turned the after galley into a bakery when at sea. The younger chaps were only just out of training and could not be trusted on their own, which meant that the Chief Cook wanted me in the galley instead of doing the baking.

By this time we had not only Naval Tailors coming on board but ordinary traders as well. They used to have Maltese lace, silks. tapestries, scarves and negligées on offer.

Another Captain's Rounds, and this time he was quite pleased. What a contrast to the *Delight*! She seemed in very bad condition and in need of a good clean-up. I went aboard her one day. Then I went ashore with Mickey Duck, an old pal from *Ganges*. We had a good look round Valetta, and noticed how there were shrines everywhere with figures of Mary in the walls. There were members of some religious order in their habits walking round with shaven heads as well as Sisters of Mercy and other nuns. We thought that the prices in the shops were much the same as at home. After having a meal of steak and chips, we met Peter and all had a drink together. A pint of Watney's Brown cost 1/6d, so after that we went on to the local brew, Blue Label and Hop Leaf, but found it inferior. We got back on board about 10 p.m. The overall impression was that this place was full of sailors!

The Landing Party side of my duties was a skylark! By the time I had got all my belts on, I looked like a flipping horse!

We had one cook on board who, to put it mildly, wasn't very clever. What a name too – Love! One night he went ashore and was not seen from then onwards. He had a wife and child too and I couldn't help thinking how hard his stupidity was making it for them. He owed money all round: one lad

£4.10s, the Doctor £9 for a camera and the tailor for two suits which he had bought.

Soon afterwards I was put on duty watch on my own, since Love had still not turned up. The Chief asked me if I could do it by myself and I thought I might as well, even though it meant giving up my afternoon at Sliema. We were carrying enough food for months ahead, but of course the fresh vegetables were brought out every week by boat and we used to take ten days' supply. We found that they didn't last that long and after two or three days we had to rely on tinned ones. Apart from this, the fresh water boat used to come out every day and fill us up. But at sea we used to make our own. Our mail was brought by BEA. We had 300 men on board and sixteen officers. We could not go alongside, which meant that going ashore meant taking either a dghaisa or a motor launch. From that particular place – but only from there – those who wanted to could have all night ashore. Not many did so.

On our last night in harbour, between 12 and 4 in the morning, we had an exercise known as 'Exercise Awkward'. Frogmen put two dummy charges underneath us, but we found them within the allotted time. We left harbour at 0900 on 18th July and anchored about four miles off St Paul's Bay. I was able to swim over the port side and it certainly freshened me up. I wrote to Pauline again asking for her form, as it had to have the Captain's signature, thereby knocking £12 off the price. After anchoring, we spent the entire day getting our guns lined up. That night we darkened ship and the next day we had gunnery practice and speed trials. It was mostly target practice and continued all week, culminating in a bombardment. The night after that we had a night exercise with *Delight*, which for some meant no sleep. The mail came aboard by landing craft. My Duty Watch went well even though I was still on my own. It used to come round every three days. However, the Chief said he would help me out. The fact that the other chap was still ashore had upset all our routine. Still he was incompetent and was not really missed. The temperature was still in excess of 100 degrees. We were back in harbour by this time, and one morning before we left an American Cruiser, the U.S.S. *Salim*, came in with the C.-in-C. of the USN 6th Fleet on board. I believe they were having a Conference at the United Nations in the course of the week. We had just got out of harbour when we passed a US Submarine going in. The following morning the US Cruiser was passing us and the tradition was that Destroyers and below piped the side and that the passing ship did the same. Everyone on the upper decks of both vessels stood to attention and we followed the rule that P.O.'s and Officers saluted Cruisers and upwards. Since we ourselves were classed as a Cruiser, the Alert was

H.M.S. Delight *in tow.*

sounded on the bugle. The US Cruiser piped 'Face right, you guys and salute your British buddies', but we thought, 'They are no buddies of ours!' As we came into harbour, the First Lieutenant was on the tannoy shouting 'Stand still, Stand still!' – and all in the terrible heat. It was only because he knew that the C.-in-C., Mediterranean was watching through his telescope. Then we had high speed trials, but the Chief gave me the afternoon off and for most of it I was asleep.

I had a chat with the Duty Officer, a Lieut-Commander, and he gave me a cigarette and asked how Pauline was doing. I mentioned the mail that kept coming from her and he asked if my messmates were jealous. I had written out a request to discontinue shaving, which meant that the following day I had to see the First Lieutenant and the day after that the Captain.

A few days later we were off St. Paul's Bay once more, playing about with the radar and towing *Delight*. The next day we were due to do gunnery exercises and test the guns and other equipment and then to repeat all the exercises again that night.

The other chap came back at last, which made life considerably easier for me, for the time being anyhow. I had no doubt that he would be off again as soon as we got in. I felt I could have no time for him. It was still as hot as ever, and each evening, on the Captain's orders, we had swimming over the side, usually between 4.30 and 5 p.m. (First Dog Watch). We hoped to be able to repeat that particular exercise next day as well, but during the day we were still chasing round the ocean.

Having done just about every possible exercise at sea, we had to do it all over again at night, as we had foreseen. It meant that I was on duty in the galley until 8 p.m. and was up again at 4 a.m. After having my tot and lunch, I tried to have a couple of hours' sleep, but I found it was too hot, In any case, by 1.30 we were Closed Up for Action Stations once more, though only for an hour. Even though we didn't actually fire, we still had to be there. Night Encounter Exercise was scheduled for that same night, and we had heard that the 4.5s would be firing star shells. They had already had a shoot that morning. All this was known as 'working up trials' and the reason that we were undergoing so extensive a range of exercises was that we were a new commission.

After the day's exercises were over, we bathed again over the side and then chucked buckets of water over one another in the showers so that once more we were nice and clean – for a short time at least. Later I was on Action Stations yet again, but was only up on deck for 10 minutes 'and So Secured'. I knew that they would be firing star shells from the Turret that evening and foresaw a couple of bulbs going, as they usually did one way or another. Fortunately the globes in which they were encased were made of strong glass. Otherwise, someone could have been blinded. I had planned to watch a film that night – *On the Waterfront.* We were on the water all right – chasing the *Delight.* Still we hoped that there would be a film the night after.

After the exercises at sea, we had anchored once more off St. Paul's Bay and the Captain's Rounds had taken place in the morning. I turned to at 7.30 a.m. and finished at 7.30 p.m. The chap who was with me made it even harder by being so slow. He saw the Captain the following day and got 10 days' scale pay and leave stopped, plus 7 days' 10, which meant more work in the mornings and afternoons as well as rifle drill. But I could have no sympathy with him. And now he started stealing! We spent the weekend at anchor. The Captain gave leave, but not many took advantage of it. I didn't know whether I would be on Divisions the next day but if I was, I would have to wear full whites. So the day before I had sewn all the badges on my suit. It took over an hour to wash and all the dye ran out of the badges. That's pussers for you! On the Wednesday we were due back in Grand Harbour and Friday was pay day.

What a day Sunday turned out to be! In the morning I had an early rise and by 9.30 was at Divisions. Prayers were held on the forecastle and afterwards the Captain spoke to us about the week's happenings. To judge from what he said, he had realised that tempers were becoming frayed at the number of things that were not working. A and X Turrets were not firing, and the same applied to Bofors and the port STAAG. As if that were not enough, we were having trouble with one of the boilers and there was something wrong with our fresh water system. However, he said, all these defects could be put right. (As late as October or November, by which time we had reached Suez, that boiler was still playing up, and in the following year fresh water was rationed and we had to wash in salt water. That, however, was still a long way ahead.)

There had been much discontent on board and it seemed to be partly the Captain's fault. We had a number of Maltese cooks and stewards but he wouldn't give them night leave. We were due to go to sea again at 5 a.m. and to do exercises all night, as we were on Night Encounter with *Delight*.

One afternoon we went sailing – three P.O.'s, seven Boys and myself. We left at 1 p.m. and were back at 5. We had a wonderful afternoon wearing just shorts and sandals and, once we were out of sight of the ship, nothing more than costumes. We went in and out of the coves, dropped anchor and went swimming and then sailed all round the bay and so on out to the little offshore islets and out to sea. There was a good wind and did we move! But how the sun caught my shoulders and legs! Still it was all good fun and certainly a change.

Soon after this we left Grand Harbour. It was 4.30 a.m. when we weighed anchor and I might as well have been up there with the Seamen who were raising the anchor. The capstan was right above our messdeck and what a row they made! We lay at anchor outside Grand Harbour from 2 p.m. that afternoon. We had been due for a torpedo shoot but it had been cancelled, as also had the Night Encounter Exercise. That morning we had fired the 4.5s at a sleeve target.

A little earlier I was talking of pilfering in connection with that useless cook I had to work with. Fortunately there was very little of it in the Navy, though of course the occasional light-fingered individual did turn up. When I was on H.M.S. *Solebay*, we had a case in which I was an actual witness and helped to get the rating involved convicted. He got 28 days' detention.

We sailed to another part of Malta and anchored off Mhurselot at 7.30 a.m. We spent another busy day firing the big guns and this time we really went to town with them. We were firing at sleeve targets and had a bombardment exercise. I cut my finger badly enough to raise the question of whether it should be stitched, but the Doctor put a type of film over it and bandaged it up. It soon became OK. According to the Petty Officer Writer, my income tax had come through and I would be getting quite a bit in the coming week.

One Seaman had an accident in which he got rope burns on both arms and legs. Actually he was lucky to get away with nothing worse. If a rope slipped, anything could happen.

All this time it was still intensely hot – so much so that I had almost forgotten what it was like to wear a shirt, except, of course, for Sunday Divisions and going ashore.

By the 27th July we found ourselves back in Grand Harbour once more, moored alongside Carradina. The temperature was over a hundred. The next morning we left the Bay at 4.30 and did some more chasing around the ocean. At 8 a.m. a helicopter landed an officer from the *Eagle* by lowering him on board by winch and at 11.30 he left the same way – because of course there wasn't room for the helicopter to land on our deck space.

After finishing work that morning I had just gone aft for a couple of hours in the sun when X Gun started a trial shoot, so instead I decided to do some dhobying, had a shower, and got some ironing done. We finished our shoot at 1 p.m. and arrived back alongside Carradina Wall in Grand Harbour by 2.30 p.m. Some work needed to be done on the boiler. As I looked round, I could see several Cruisers in harbour as well as some American vessels, an Italian Cruiser and a New Zealand Aircraft Carrier.

We were due to go to Venice in September, which was about a month later than had originally been planned. By this time a free laundry had been started on board and we were able to get our aprons and blue shorts washed. I was still borrowing a bathing costume from the Chief Cook and decided that I must get one of my own. I was planning to get some more sailing in the following Sunday, and to organise some 'big eats' for all concerned.

According to the *Malta Times*, that week had been the hottest for ten years, which was saying something! The temperature rose to 115° and 105° in the shade. Sprays were put on the upper deck so as to cool the messdecks. It was rumoured that we were to go to Cyprus to relieve H.M.S. *Crossbow*.

One night we had a film show on the Upper Deck and it was quite good. Also we had figs for sweet, so I saved some of the juice and put it in the fridge. This meant that we could have fig juice at the pictures. It was a practice of ours with all tinned fruit. We used to strain the juice off and put it in the fridge for us chefs. Healthy kids – that's what we were!

Our visit to Venice was postponed from August 1st to some time in September. One of the chefs, Parsons by name, went down with tonsillitis and bronchitis. He went to hospital with 'Happy' Day, the seaman who had the accident and got rope burns. A few days later we were storing ship. We were going to Cyprus to relieve *Crossbow*, which was already there. Such at least was the most recent buzz. I was doubtful whether we would be sailing so soon. The whaler was still on board and now that we were alongside the wall, couldn't be lowered. I found that the apricot juice was too rich; after all, it came from about 20 lbs of apricots! So I diluted it with water.

While we were still alongside the wall, Pauline's letter arrived with the form for a reduction in the fare for the flight out to Malta. I gave it to my Divisional Officer, who got the Captain to sign it. I then posted it back to Pauline.

Our Fleet mail was all carried from Sicily by a yacht named *The Star of Malta*, carrying passengers and mail. But then one night all the papers and parcels arrived soaked through. She had run on to some rocks in a mist, gone aground, and turned on her side. All the passengers got off safely, I believe, but it would be some time before she resumed her task of carrying mail from Sicily.

At last the temperature fell, if only to 90°. After the intense heat we had endured for so long, it felt quite pleasant! By this time we were due to go to sea again for 21 days accompanying the *Eagle* and also some of the American Fleet. Bank Holiday came round but I found myself on Duty Watch, which was unlucky. The day after this we moved berth back to our old place at Senglea, opposite St. Angelo.

The next day we were off to sea again in company with H.M.S. *Eagle* and H.M.S. *Sheffield*, with a fair number of exercises ahead of us. We anchored overnight in St. Paul's Bay. This put paid to our plans for sailing on Sunday.

By 3rd August, 1955, plans had changed yet again. That morning we left harbour about seven am and spent most of the day chasing. I was at Action Stations and aircraft from the *Eagle* were up, so we had never a dull moment and were firing pretty constantly. That evening we dropped anchor at last. The Duty Officer saw me that morning and asked me whether we had Cleared Lower Deck. I replied that I had not and that we never did so, but he said that from then on we would be having to. They used not to bother us with such details as a rule.

I had some mail from Pauline, the mail having been delivered by jackstay from *Delight*. Early the next morning we left, with about nine visiting officers from various nations aboard, for another shoot. Soon after returning to Grand Harbour, we left again at five for St. Paul's Bay, where we would be staying for a few days. The next day I was on duty on my own again. A few weeks before, the Chief had decided to close the galley for cooking and it was only being used for preparing the vegetables and, when necessary, for baking at night. However, the Seamen who were preparing the vegetables

The Education Officer.

were not keeping it clean. As a result, the Chief decided to resume cooking there and put two chefs in, leaving four others for the forrard galley. We were still one cook short until the one in hospital was discharged. Then I was due to go on day work again. The next day we moved into Grand Harbour once more. A number of defects had been revealed, especially in the guns and the boilers, and they would all have to be repaired before we went to sea again.

By this time it was early August and one Sunday morning we were entering Grand Harbour. I had to fall in on B Gun Deck in No. 6 full whites. The night before, the Daily Orders had stated that the Captain wanted a smart ship to enter harbour. By the time we arrived, it was stated, the ships already in would be on Sunday Divisions. Yet when we did get in, there wasn't a darned ship in sight!

That afternoon seven of us went sailing and had a nice afternoon with a picnic of ham and tomato sandwiches which I had prepared. We went up Sliema Creek. When we arrived in Grand Harbour, the Captain noticed that so many of us were not wearing the dress of the day that he sent the First Lieutenant round the messes to put all offenders in the rattle. That upset everyone again but he didn't catch me. One A/B came back from ashore with a canary, which was against regulations: no pets allowed on board.

However, we did have a kitten which someone had brought on board and nothing had been said so far. The Captain of the *Delight* had a parrot, and on that ship anyone could have what they liked.

At that time we had three lads on board who were on open arrest, though all on different charges. One engine room mechanic had sworn at the Gunnery Officer. A Seaman had been cheeky to the Officer of the Watch while in the dghaisa, and had remained ashore even though he had been told to come back. And finally the cook, Love, who had already given so much trouble, had gone ashore and with his past record, heaven knew whether he would be back.

I was still the butt of jokes and ribbing about the length of Pauline's letters. 'What you got there, Joe, a book?' 'Is the library open yet?' I just used to grin and say that there was no need to be jealous. By this time my locker was getting filled with these letters from my young wife, but I was reluctant to sort them out or dispose of any of them. She also used to send magazines, which were very welcome and much looked forward to.

The dates for our Adriatic cruise had now been officially published. We were to leave Malta on the 29th August, arriving at Venice on 1st September and remaining there until the 7th, when we would be going to Split in Yugoslavia. After a day there, we would be going to Dubrovnik, arriving there on 12th and leaving on the 15th, so as to arrive back in Malta on the 16th. Then on the 29th we were to leave for Naples, arriving there on 30th and leaving on 3rd of October so as to be back in Malta the following day. As it turned out, we didn't exactly follow this itinerary, especially so far as the visit to Yugoslavia was concerned. We were due to start a refit on the 24th October, but were to get in some time before. Pauline, we hoped, would be arriving on 21st, and we would already be in harbour by then.

The Aircraft Carrier *Albion* arrived and was to relieve *Eagle*, so we expected to be doing exercises with her.

In the cookery department we were more or less back to normal, though the Chief Cook wasn't well and was suffering from an ulcer. We were to sail on the Monday and come in on Friday, having had plenty of gun trials and Night Encounters in the meantime. The Duty Officer gave me some useful advice about Pauline's visit. He said it would be better if she came for a month and suggested that she should ask for that much leave from work. 'Not from Fleetwood House!', I replied, but then he said that she could always get another job. When Pauline did arrive, I hoped to get 7 days' leave, but this was still uncertain.

After a good afternoon's swimming and lazing on the beach at Melhiaha Bay, we got a bus through St. Paul's Bay and came back to Valetta, where we had 'big eats': steak, chips and sauerkraut, beetroot, fried onions and peas.

A new regulation was issued stating that from then on I and the other Supply and Secretariat would have to fall in on B Gun Deck for Leaving Harbour and also for Entering. All the guns had been fired and I heard that the ship was now considered free of its former defects. We anchored at St. Paul's Bay at 12 noon and left at 7 p.m. to do an exercise and fire starshell. As from Wednesday of that week I was on day work. Parsons was back and was to take my place. Thus my hours were now 8 a.m. to 3.30 p.m., but even then the Chief was continually changing the routine.

We left next morning and were firing everything that could be fired: torpedoes, guns etc. The bombardment was still continuing and we didn't expect to anchor before 11 p.m. that night. When A Turret was firing from just above us, the smell of cordite was horrible. There would be a mighty wham, everything would shake and the bulbs used to go out. Down would come cups, cap boxes and anything else that happened to be hanging, and the rum fanny used to hit the deck more often than anything else. This went on unceasingly. We kept hanging things up only to have them come down all over again. For the first time since arriving in Malta we had a few spits of rain, though it never came to anything. In the evening we headed for Grand Harbour, where we were to anchor for the night. But the next morning we were due to leave early, with a heavy programme of firing still to complete.

Still we were trying to get the guns right and, in the process, doing a lot of firing. The following Saturday, according to the Night's Orders, we would be taking a Marine Band to Messina.

Often I had to be on Starboard STAAG, which certainly didn't please the Chief Cook, and in addition I was down for Entering Harbour again. The First Lieutenant went down with 'Malta Dog', a kind of dysentery which may have been caused by the water and the Captain was not very well either. Another officer was in hospital with some kind of fever.

A few days later we had yet another shoot, opening up with STAAG and Bofors, so we had a terrible racket going on for a while. However, no cooks were required and we missed Entering Harbour as well. Some film people had come on board and were taking shots of us and our activities. At last a good thunderstorm came and we had a real downpour for a time – the first since arriving in Malta.

We had another marvellous afternoon with a group of the lads, who included the Coder, Ben, Jack Dusty and myself. The Coder, I should explain, used to help the Education Officer and assist with official documents. We used to share him and the Doctor with H.M.S. *Delight*. Just as we were on the point of stepping into the dghaisa to set out, the Gunnery Officer and the Medical Officer came along. We stood back to let them go first but they said, 'Come on, we might as well all go together' and paid for the boat themselves. We had a smashing afternoon at Melhiaha playing and larking around with a 3/6d beach ball which we had bought. We got back on board about 9.30 and I then had a terrific headache caused by too much skylarking and also by being too long in the sun.

By this time news had come through that we were not going to Yugoslavia after all. The King of Greece was going and we didn't want to coincide with his visit. As a result, we were due to spend ten days in Venice and then to go on to Ancona, which was a seaside resort.

By now things had settled down well in the galley and the Chief Cook was more and more ready to leave me to work on my own and in my own way. Also, being in port, the ship was quite steady, which made work in the galley much easier. The food was exceptionally good, especially the meat, though it was not always possible to choose what we wanted. Another minor problem was that some of the food had to be bought ashore and although the provisioners did their best, it was not invariably of the best quality.

At the next pay day we were told that we would have only £4, which came to 5000 lira, to spend ashore in Venice. There were 20 in the mess and two Leading Cooks and two assistants. A Maltese barber came aboard and I took the opportunity to have my beard trimmed and a haircut. He had a cheek, though. He used to go from ship to ship and whichever suited him best, he would get permission to stay on her as barber. He was certainly on to a good thing! He had just got back from the South of France and the Italian Riviera. However, he couldn't come with us because his wife wouldn't let him.

The *Delight* and the *Sheffield* were to accompany us to Venice, so we foresaw that it would be like Chatham Barracks.

I was baking once more. The other cook had been moaning about having to do it at night, so we arranged that I would do it one night and he the next. Once we got to Venice, the baking would be done on the *Sheffield*, and she wanted to borrow a cook from us. We decided to let them have Love, who was useless anyway. During my night shift I made one dough and left it proving in the bin until 9.30. Then I made a second and at 11.30 I moulded it up to prove it. Both doughs were just right and I got them into the oven. All this made the baking far easier and I was very pleased with the result. By the time the night was over, I had done about 200 lbs of bread with no trouble. This was especially good in view of the smallness of the galley, which meant that the bread had to be made and baked in relays.

A Seaman who went ashore on Friday came back 30-odd hours adrift. Our programme included plenty of exercises once we left harbour, and many of these had to be undertaken with the *Birmingham* and five other ships. The *Sheffield* was due to join us but we heard that she had some trouble and might not be able to take part in many exercises.

The order for 'Darkened Ship' was piped, and for the first part of the exercise we were trying to find some submarines, which would almost certainly take several hours. Fortunately I was not involved because I had another batch of bread to bake and also had to give the Chief a hand with the weighing and moulding.

Next night I did go up to the Gun Deck and found that we were going to be attacked by Italian MTBs. That should prove interesting, I thought, but I didn't have time to stay up there and had to return to my baking. There was a full moon, which increased their chances of finding us first. This skylark continued till midnight, and the teams would be going into Action Stations at 4 a.m.! Then at 9 there was to be a mass attack by Italian fighters dive-bombing. As if that were not enough, the C.-in-C. was due to transfer to us from the *Sheffield* by jackstay. I was up and in the galley from 8 a.m. until 10.30, and at 11.30 I drew the rum and had my own tot. After that I had lunch and got my head down until 3 p.m., when I had a cup of tea before going to Evening Quarters. I also got in a lot of dhobying.

CHAPTER VI

Venice and Ancona

WE ARRIVED IN VENICE on the 1st September, 1955. We were lying in the harbour accompanied by the *Sheffield*, *Delight* and *Surprise*. At the first opportunity we went ashore, using our own boats; the gondolas were too expensive! We landed in the Piazza San Marco and began to explore from there. In and out of shops we went, up narrow streets, over the many little bridges. We saw a great number and variety of musical instruments but at last we got a bit leg-weary and returned to the Piazza San Marco. While we were having a humble coca cola at one of the big restaurants there, one of our party, Rick by name, had the cheek to ask the waiter where we could get a decent meal at a reasonable price. He took us round the back of the Piazza and showed us a place where we had a smashing meal, with soup, chicken, chips and peas and a bottle of wine. After that we returned to the Piazza and sat listening to the orchestra and watching the crowds. Visitors of every conceivable nationality were to be seen, especially, I suppose, because of the Film Festival which was being held at the time. We caught the boat back at 11 p.m.

The following Thursday we were at sea when the C.-in-C. came to visit us, landing by jackstay. After looking us over, he returned to the *Sheffield* by the same route. It all looked quite easy really.

Pauline wrote to say that the Navy was to be cut but I replied that according to the sources in the Mediterranean Fleet, it had already been cut by half over the past two years.

She had also asked how many cabins the Captain had and I told her two, a day and a night one. The night cabin was near the Bridge, so he used to use it all the time.

One of our chefs, Derby by name, decided to go and see the local festival, which included a gondola race on the Grand Canal and a procession of boats decorated with flowers.

One morning while we were at Venice, the Duty Officer asked the Chief Cook whether the two Leading Hands had passed for Petty Officer. When the Chief told him they had not, he said that we could both prepare for the exam. in refit time. 'Here we go again', I said to myself, 'Out with the books once more!' There was a cookery school in Malta, so we thought we would probably be going there.

Soon after this I went on a tour of a glass factory. Twenty hands went from the *Sheffield*, another twenty from the *Delight* and twenty from ourselves. Our first stop was at one of the larger islands and in we went to our first glass factory, where we watched the craftsmen blowing and blending in the various colours they used. They made figurines of such objects as pheasants etc. We also saw the furnaces where the molten glass was produced. After that we spent about one and a half hours touring the little bridges and streets, which I found especially interesting. Here in the north of Italy Communism was quite strong, and when we passed a Communist Centre, we booed it. It was in a pretty dilapidated area and the Hammer and Sickle emblem was rather crude. After we had left the larger island we sailed to a smaller one, where there was a little fishing village. We landed at the side of a bridge and immediately children swarmed all over us. We had a good wander round and caused quite a stir. People kept shaking hands with us and we were struck by the number of priests, many of them wearing long beards. We were also able to see inside some of the homes, which, although somewhat run down on the outside, on the inside, by contrast, were spotless. From there we sailed for a smaller island still, where an ancient church had been turned into a museum. It was full of marble tombs and shrines of popes and saints many hundreds of years old, as well as numerous works of art.

After that we returned to the Grand Canal, Venice's main thoroughfare. The traffic here reminded us of the A1. There were waterbuses and gondolas pulling in at landing stages along the route. We were in the limelight and I suppose that sixty sailors, all in whites on an open boat, did look somewhat conspicuous. All day people were waving to us. When we passed a boat with a Yank in it, accompanied by two girls, we blew raspberries at him – what a rotten lot we were, but it made the girls laugh! The opera houses, consulates and museums were all along this route and when we reached the British Consulate, we gave the flag three rousing cheers. Someone came out on the balcony and laughed his head off. Then when we were passing the American Embassy we all blew raspberries again. All in all it was good fun and a thoroughly good day. We returned under the Bridge of Sighs and got back to the ship about 5 p.m.

A large group of film stars were supposed to be coming to visit the ship as the Captain's guests but they failed to turn up. The Film Festival was being held at the Lido at a sort of open-air cinema where new films were shown every night – French, Italian, British – from all nationalities. Each day about 17 free tickets were sent to our ship, but in view of the limited number, we had to draw for them. Pauline's heart-throb was here, namely Edmund Purdon. One Wednesday the ship was open to visitors and the following

Friday we parted company with *Sheffield* and *Surprise*, which were returning to Malta. The *Delight* and ourselves were to go on to Ancona before likewise returning to Malta four days later. We would be there for three days, followed by a week on exercises at sea, and after that we would be going to Naples. This programme was, of course, provisional and subject to alteration.

One evening about 6.30, while we were still in Venice, Edmund Purdon and Lynda Christine came on board. At the time I was working in the galley and out of the rig of the day, so I didn't get to the Upper Deck to see them. The next day, however, I had better luck when they piped a boat full of film stars approaching the ship. The party included James Robertson Justice, Jack Hawkins (who is really a very big man) and Donald Sinden, both the two last-named having been in *The Cruel Sea*. I had a chat with James Robertson Justice about falconry. Among the ladies were Belinda Lee, Eunice Grayson and Mary Ure. Those women smelt like florists and were wearing makeup as thick as plaster. Although the ship was pretty crowded by this time, they all posed for photographs.

A day or two later we heard that plans had been altered yet again. From Ancona we would be going on exercises and then on to Gibraltar. From there we would be visiting Algeria and then Naples, and so back to Malta, where we were due to arrive on the 19th October. Later still I heard that we would also be visiting Cyprus, but, as it later turned out, it was only Gibraltar and Algeria after all. I didn't forget for one moment that Pauline was due to arrive in Malta on 21st October.

Our time in Venice was now up and we were due to sail for Ancona, first refuelling from a tanker. We would be arriving, we were told, at 9 a.m. Since I was off watch the day we were leaving Venice, I thought I might get roped in for Leaving Harbour. I didn't mind all that much, except for the inconvenience of changing into full whites. Love, the chef whom we had loaned to the *Sheffield*, was due to rejoin us the day we left. The Chief Baker on *Sheffield* sent a highly sarcastic message to our Chief Cook saying, 'Thanks for sending your best hand'. I would be baking again on Sunday night and Derby was due to make one dough on Sunday. We would be baking on our own for several days. Although *Delight* would be with us, she would be doing her own baking.

We arrived in Ancona on 11th September, 1955. Quite a large crowd gathered to look at us and even more came that afternoon. We were warned not to go ashore on our own and not to go to dances, as dance halls were all controlled by the Communists. As time went on, we felt that people were not much interested in us. This could partly have been due to the language barrier but there was more to it than that. It became clear that the

Communists had considerable power in all departments of life. We walked around, bought and devoured a huge slice of melon apiece, and watched a Punch and Judy show in Italian. But the overall impression was somewhat depressing and the Ship's Company were not very impressed with Ancona. The people seemed cowed. My moustache, with its waxed ends, attracted a lot of attention.

All this time I was hoping to get to Malta to be ready for Pauline's arrival but couldn't find anyone to change with me so that I could finish my time there.

The *Delight* was lying opposite to us but had developed a leak in one of her fuel tanks. This caused her to alter her programme and leave for Malta the next day, whereas we would be staying a few days longer. On one day the ship was open to visitors, but only to those who had an official pass. We had a group of eight or nine scouts from Malta on board, and they had booked a bus to take them to some shrine. Any of us who wanted to could accompany them. True Roman Catholics that they were, they presented the ship with the image of a saint.

Ken, the Seaman who lost his watch, came back one night and it was obvious that he had been fighting. He had gone ashore with five others but was unable to say where they were. Then Mick, the other Leading Cook, was brought back in a police van but Derby, Smudge and Charlie were still unaccounted for. When they did finally turn up, Derby and Ken were put in the rattle and quite a few others turned up the worse for wear after escapades ashore.

I managed to bake a good batch of bread but how much easier it would have been if the P.O. Stores and a Chief had not been getting in the way! They were in the galley making sandwiches and tea for themselves. I resolved that next time I was baking, I would lock the door! On another morning, about 2 a.m., a Quartermaster and I were talking to a policeman. He came on board and had a cup of tea with us. With the help of three pairs of hands, we had a conversation about motor scooters. Lambrettas, we discovered, were made partly here and partly in Germany. Vespas were particularly popular, but scooters in general were in demand. We asked whether the Commies caused a lot of trouble and he told us that things were gradually improving. The Commies, he said, were on the way out, though in certain departments they still exercised considerable power. In having such a conversation we were certainly taking a chance. He could so well have been a Communist himself!

We thought that the post office at Ancona must be one of those departments that were Commie-controlled. Instead of delivering our mail to us here at Ancona, they had sent it on to Malta! As far as work was concerned, by now it was going quite well. I used to work on my own, which always suited me better, and it used to go smoothly. The Chief Cook had come to trust me and leave me to whatever job I thought wanted doing.

Unfortunately it was pouring with rain when four bus-loads of school-children came to see the ship. Alas, regulations meant that we couldn't let them on board.

I thought it was time I told Pauline about some of the people I was living with, their personalities and qualifications. I lived with them in No. 11 Mess, so decided to describe them in order. First there was Ken, a Leading Seaman and the 'Killick' of the Mess. He had been on *Solebay* with me and was the one who lost his watch. Another Leading Seaman was Hick – short for Hickling – who was the postman of the ship and the first man to step ashore after we had secured. The other Leading Cook was Mick, whose real name was Roy Mickel. I knew him from the old days. Pedro was an A.B. who was in charge of the paint shop and who also liked dominoes. Those were the more senior of the hands, but there were a number of very junior ones as well, some of them being at sea for the first time. Ben Norris was quite a comic, Wally could be classed as somewhat quiet, 'Doctor' Rees was another Seaman, while Eddie was a bit of a know-all and none too popular. Another guy, Pete, used to write home to his wife every night and did not go ashore at either Venice or Ancona. Another know-all, and not particularly clean either, was a man named Shaw. He used to get told off enough! Love was a man I have already described and he continued to be useless and incompetent, so that I constantly had to carry him. Another of the chefs was Derby, who I thought must be a woman-hater as well as a drink-lover. In another ten years, I thought, he would be an old man. O'Connor and Henty were junior seamen and as such used to get all the work in the mess, such as making the tea etc. They always used to look after us four first . . . or else there would have been trouble! The rest were seamen and in any case worked in different parts of the ship. Carter was what was known as a Tanky. He used to get stores up from below and help the Storeman. Finally, of course, there was myself, who used to write to his wife every night – a good job too, or all this would never have been set down on paper!

One Saturday, as soon as possible after we were due to arrive in Malta, I planned to go ashore and look at a flat in Senglea which we were hoping to rent, and to make all necessary arrangements.

We had sailed from Ancona by this time and were in the Mediterranean, having left the coast of Sicily at 11 a.m. that morning. We had left the murky grey, the aftermath of a storm, and were once more in the blue. I was in the galley by eight and was due back again there by four to prepare rissoles for supper. We were not far from Malta, where we would be arriving a little before nine, but would have to lie at anchor outside the harbour since there was a rule that no one could enter at night.

We now had firm information that we would be arriving in Malta on the 19th, a Wednesday morning, and that we would be going into drydock on the 24th. The following Monday we would be going to sea and were due to have about ten to twelve days of exercises. We would probably be calling in to Gibraltar to fuel and then going on to Algeria.

Once arrived in Malta, we found ourselves once more enduring pretty fierce heat, though thank goodness, it was cooler at night. We were to begin a major exercise on the Monday, in which French, Dutch and Belgian ships would be taking part. The exercise consisted of screening a convoy and the French were to be in charge. The NATO regulations decreed that each nation in turn had to take the lead.

The Chief Cook was leaving us, which meant that for the time being I had no duties, but there would be a lot of baking to be done. We arranged that I would do one night's baking and Derby the other. I saw that the film *Doctor at Sea* won the award at the Venice Film Festival. Ken got one day's pay and seven days' leave stopped. He was made an example of as he was a Leading Seaman.

At 8.25 on the 18th September we left for ten days at sea. We were heading towards Gibraltar, which meant that we would be a few hundred miles nearer home. I heard that we might be anchoring for the night and refuelling at one or two places, but that, in true Naval tradition, we would be having plenty of sea-time. Rick was in the Mess opposite, consisting of 19, while our Mess had 20. There we used to eat, sleep, iron and play games, discuss the Captain and swear terribly. The point is that living with men at close quarters all the time, you couldn't help getting into their ways. Still you had to be careful about the swearing; I recognised that bad language was nothing to be proud of.

Flats were easy to get in Malta, as so many had been left vacant. The *Sheffield* and *Cumberland* were both due to leave for home, with the result that practically no ships were left in Malta. *Delight* and ourselves were to put to sea the next day. That left only the fourth Submarine Depot Ship, which was in Malta permanently, and one 'Aisne' Battle Class Destroyer.

We left Grand Harbour at 9.30 a.m. on 19th, and set course for Arzie, a place in French North Africa where we were due to anchor the following night. We were to join up with a French Cruiser there and start 'Exercise Medflex' in company with the *Delight*. We were the only British ships taking part. No leave was to be given until we reached Naples, and we heard that we would be fuelling at 6 a.m. and doing a bombardment off a point at Sardinia. We would also be going to Gibraltar for three hours to fuel. Little O'Connor, one of the Junior Seamen, had a mishap while skylarking which reduced him to tears. He was a nice kid and I was genuinely sorry. The rest, I felt, might be taking it easy on him from then on, as he was on the small side and no match for them.

By this time we could see the coast of Africa but, as somebody asked, where were the lions? The Chief Cook wanted to see me after the film last night and he asked me to turn out with the duty cook so as to get ahead with the dinner. At 8.30 the following morning I saw the First Lieutenant and had also to see the Captain for his approval of my going through for P.O. You had to go through the proper channels to make sure that you could be spared. My Divisional Supply Officer told me that it had been recommended and that was it!

At 9 a.m. Action Stations was piped. Half an hour later we had the signal for gas, so I had to put on my respirator for a further half hour. I managed to get back to the galley by 10.30 and it was as well that we were ahead with the preparations; otherwise lunch would have been really late. At Evening Quarters we had all sorts of exercises, such as fires in various parts of the ship, wearing respirators again and MEs taking the seaboat away. The next day we would be doing a shoot and 'Control Parties Close Up' and 'Director Crews'.

That morning a flying fish – the first I had seen – landed on the Quarter Deck. It had quite a span of wings; they were longer than its body. The Divisional Officer asked whether Pauline would be coming that day and I replied that she would not, as she could get only a week's holiday. He said it really wasn't good enough of the Amalgamated Press and told me that there was a good job going for a secretary in the Supply Department of the Admiralty here. Furthermore it would be for an Englishwoman, as they did not, I believe, take any Maltese for jobs of this kind.

No less than four exercises were going on in the Med. at the same time and the one we were taking part in was under the command of a French Carrier. We had mock gas and atomic attacks again, but I was excused. The Chief was granted permission for this by the DO. This officer was all right but, like so many others, dead scared of the Captain.

The sea was as flat as a duck pond and I made two doughs. By this time we were getting close to Gibraltar and there was some mist to contend with. Round Malta, by contrast, it was quite clear. This was the season for migrating birds, and some of the migrants used to land exhausted on the ships and, I am sorry to say, didn't have the strength to continue their journey. Next morning I was due to see the Captain about going through for P.O. but it was just a formality. I knew I would have to get my books out again and that there would be a lot of studying to be done. You had to know what went on in a cake when it was in the oven, study minerals and types of flour, as well as the various types of ovens, ways to arrange the bread in the oven, different sizes of tins and how to write out menus. In addition I would have an essay to write and would have to stand up in front of those on the course and give a running commentary on a brine tub or cleanliness in the galley. I was determined to do my best, but did not have much confidence that I would be a P.O. as there were too many on the roster. If I did get through, it would mean 1/6d a day extra.

On the 22nd September we were at sea when Action Stations was piped yet again. The noise increased from then on. I was on Captain's request and had to get into my No. 10 dress. My request was that during our re-fit I should attend the Cookery School in Malta. I did not consider that the 1/6d a day would help all that much, but if I managed to get the rate, my pay would go up by 5/- a day and that would make a deal of difference.

Early the next morning we put into Gibraltar, which meant that we would be getting mail and also bread. After Captain's Request I changed back, had a tot, and went to sleep in the sun on X Gun Deck. The *Daring*, the other ship in the group in Malta, was due into Gibraltar the next day on her way out and after a few weeks working up, was due to join us. When we went into Gibraltar that morning it was to take on oil and the mail was there waiting for us and also the bread. Once we had been fixed up, it was out to sea again.

The exercise in which we were now engaged was due to be carried on right through the weekend and the following day we had yet again to endure the gas and atomic attack drill which we had already been through twice. This time, unfortunately, I was not excused. During the mock gas attack we all had to wear respirators for a couple of hours. I finished work in the galley at 12 but was due to bake again that same night.

We next had a Night Encounter exercise with an Italian Cruiser and Destroyers and next day we had a bombardment off the southern coast of Sardinia. We were expecting to enter Cagliari and although we knew no leave would be granted, we were hoping for mail there. We left Cagliari in the early morning and proceeded anti-clockwise around Malta and back to Sicily. What we were to do there I didn't know, but we were due to arrive in Naples on 30th. The sea was rather choppy all day and grew rougher by nightfall – enough to upset some. The worst sailors were the Maltese. The ship had only to roll once, we found, and they were laid low. They used to live on toast. That night they had an emergency on the *Delight* and came alongside for the Doctor. He went over by jackstay and stayed on her for the rest of the night, returning in the morning. They also had someone landed by helicopter and taken off by the same means. The French were a bit jittery. They issued a general order that we were not to go any closer to them by night. I believed they might have been frightened of a collision.

On the 25th September we found ourselves still screening the Carriers miles out to sea. The exercise was due to finish at midnight and another would be starting almost at once, this time with the Italians taking part. By now the sea was less choppy, though there was still quite a swell and also an underwater tow, so that as we were moving at speed, we were experiencing a steady roll.

I had already made my doughs and would be starting to bake just after 10 p.m. Just after 10 a.m. I finished work in the galley and had my tot and lunch.

After the bombardment in which we were taking part, we were due to go into harbour. I doubted whether leave would be granted, though once more we were all hoping for mail. I had already been to Sardinia on an occasion when the kids had stoned the lads of our crew. They seemed to have taken a dislike to us. To our disappointment, no mail had arrived for us.

A few nights later, at about 2.30 a.m., we had a Night Encounter with an Italian Cruiser. The French Carrier which was on our side sent us and the *Delight* into the attack and then turned and withdrew! The Italian ship, *Abruzzi* by name, then sank us and damaged the *Delight*. Her guns had a longer range than ours and she was much faster. No guns were fired but that's how it goes when you have to rely on radar to tell you the different positions, ranges, etc.

On Monday morning *Abruzzi*, *Delight* and ourselves had another bombardment off the coast of Sardinia and after that we went back in to Cagliari, arriving about 5.30 p.m. The first ashore was the postman but the post office was closed. The Captain gave leave for a few hours and although Derby was on duty, he was eager to get ashore so I agreed to take his place. I made another dough for him and at 10 p.m., when he came back, I had one batch ready for the oven. I left it to him and he put it in the oven, moulded up another batch, and then went to sleep. The result was that he burnt the first lot and over-proved the second. I don't know how he got out of that one! Every time I did a favour for someone, I used to get let down. I think the Chief Cook found a way out of it. It all got eaten and there were no complaints except from the fish! Postie went ashore again the next morning but returned without so much as an envelope! That meant that there would be no mail for us until we reached Naples. At 10.30 we left without the *Delight*, which had developed some sort of trouble and had to stay for another two days. We were accompanying the *Abruzzi*. I was rum bosun again, so at 11.30 we had wets all round and after lunch I got my head down till five. That night I made two doughs together and a third an hour later.

By this time we had embarked on another Nato exercise, this time proceeding round Malta in an anti-clockwise direction. A trip to Rome for an audience with the Pope was organised for the R.C.'s. It cost 24 shillings. I didn't think much of Cagliari. It was a large harbour and a biggish town, but those who went ashore didn't like it. The Communists were, of course, very strong in Sardinia.

By the 29th September we were at sea again. The weather was pretty rough and we were not allowed on the Upper Deck. Our bows were digging deep and the oggin was rushing along the deck. I finished work at about 3.30 a.m. but spent some time cleaning up and having a shower, so that it was nearly 5 by the time I turned in. We stopped for about half an hour just outside Grand Harbour. The *Abruzzi* had some English students aboard whom she had to land at Malta. I received the magazines but no letters, so by the time we reached Naples I would be looking forward to a real bumper packet. I was finding great difficulty in writing because the ship was rolling and pitching so much. A table and stool had already gone flying, to say nothing of a couple of cups, but there had been no real damage. In weather like this I used to change my drink from tea with tinned milk (not very nice) to Oxo. By Tuesday the weather had worsened again and we had to pack in the exercise. Conditions were pretty uncomfortable by midnight. We were heaving around pretty violently and various utensils and items of furniture were flying about. The best way to try and sleep under these conditions was to lie as still as possible but by that time it was quite beyond me even to attempt it. I wasn't looking forward to the baking which I was due to do that night either! At last we made it to Naples and secured bow and stern, so we could settle down again.

We got in about 12 a.m., passing Cape Vesuvius and Sorrento as we did so. I was not required to go on deck for Entering Harbour. The postie went ashore and we all eagerly looked forward to him coming back laden with our long-overdue mail. I was expecting to go ashore myself about four that afternoon and was hoping to get some postcards for Pauline, have a look round and perhaps get a glass of chianti or vermouth. I had set myself a limit of 2,000 lire.

When I did get ashore, I was with one of the stokers, who, like myself, was bearded. It was a case of two black beards together. It had been pouring with rain and once again the wind was getting up and the weather was threatening. As soon as we got outside the gate, half the population of Naples were there wanting to guide us round. We got rid of all of them except one, who hung on. I had promised to get one of my mates a musical box.

The chap who had insisted on coming with us took us to a little shop in a back street, where I managed to get a very smart one. We decided to return on board with it; we didn't want to have to carry it round with us and apart from that, we wanted to get rid of that bum. So a little later we went ashore again, this time walking behind the Chief Cook and the Chief Stores. Sure enough, no sooner had they reached the gates than they were swooped on by about six at once, all wanting to sell them watches in exchange for English sterling and cigarettes – the Italians used to 'go a bundle' on those. Anyway, by this time the two Chiefs were getting seriously annoyed, so we all jumped into a taxi and made for a bar which they knew from of old. They had arranged to meet two other Chiefs there and the Chief Cook wanted to buy me a drink. But blow me if one of those damned bums hadn't jumped into the taxi with us! Anyway, the Chief bought me a vermouth and I bought him an anisette (which tastes like aniseed) and we had a natter. Then we moved on. As we were walking down the street, we were constantly being pestered. Everyone was trying to sell us something. In one shop I bought some postcards and a small present for Pauline and had a look at some jewellery. It was far too expensive, however. After wandering round a few more shops, we went to a night club – the first I had ever visited. It was quite good too. We had a beer and got talking to some French sailors, whose ship was on the other side of the harbour next to the *Abruzzi*. After that we came back on board. That evening the Chief came to see me. He told me that for the trip to Rome the next day, we would have to prepare bag meals, which meant that we had 50 pasties to prepare. I had to get cracking at once to get it all done. The party for Rome was due to leave at 5 a.m. the next morning, and by this time it was about 9.30 p.m. in the evening.

I was busy answering Pauline's letters and was still trying to persuade her to come to Malta while the ship was in drydock. But the people she was working for wouldn't give her the time off and in addition we were having to watch our finances. (In the end, though, she did come for a fortnight and ended up staying three months!) She had the offer of a job with the Admiralty and I tried to change ship to one which would be staying for a longer commission. How different it all was to the time when I was trying to get to the same depot at Chatham! I heard of a job as Leading Cook on the *Forth*, so I went over to her only to find that there was no one in the galley, it being a Sunday afternoon. I snagged my best suit on a table, found the mess at last and had a word with the Leading Cook, but all in vain. By that time he had changed his mind.

We left Naples on 20th September and I was on deck dressed in my best for Leaving Harbour. With our official bugles and pipes, we were pretty smart as we passed all those French and Italian warships. I was sorry to have been unable to visit Capri. That day I was on duty in the galley. We had FO2 on board, which always used to cause a panic.

We arrived back in Malta on Tuesday, 4th October, 1955. I still had not finished answering Pauline's letters. We, together with *Delight*, were to have six days in harbour before going back to sea again the following Monday. We were supposed to go to Algiers and spend three days there and three days on the voyage back. That would put us back in Malta for the 19th, after de-ammunitioning and de-oiling before going into drydock. I had a talk with my boss D.O. one afternoon. I asked whether I could have a week's leave if my wife could come to Malta. 'Certainly,' he said, 'that's been arranged for a long time.' I wouldn't have minded betting that the Chief had something to do with it. On the Friday, which was pay day, I had made up my mind to go ashore and look at some flats in either Senglea or Valetta. If Pauline was unable to come after all, I could always cancel. I had no baking to do at this time and was on day-work, finishing each day about 3.30. I needed to get my kit sorted out. I was back in white shorts and shirts and blue trousers to go ashore.

The next day we had a shoot and also fired torpedoes, and I heard that it went particularly well. The shoot was only three minutes slower than the record, which meant that we had to achieve both accuracy on target and as many shots fired as we could get in in the quickest time. That was why three weeks of trials were necessary. The *Daring* was undergoing the same exercise, though where, precisely, we had no means of knowing.

The *Birmingham* came in on the Wednesday, followed by *Striker* and *Reggio*. A big Cunard liner named the *Carronia* also came into harbour. She had been on a cruise with, I believed, just over 500 passengers aboard.

The Chief Cook had some close acquaintances ashore and, by a stroke of luck, had been able to fix up flats for some of his chums whose wives were coming out. He said he would see what he could do for me.

I wished they would pipe the postman to lay aft. Then we would know whether there was any chance of some mail.

At last something was being done about our mail. A signal was sent to the C.-in-C. to say that it was adrift. *Delight* was getting hers so none of us could understand what had happened to ours. It was not at Naples either. Then a signal came through from the GPO in London to say that it had been held

Our billet in Malta.

up there. At this stage I was still trying to organise a flat for Pauline's visit to Malta.

We left harbour about 8 a.m. and then did a defective torpedo shoot. Apparently, something was wrong with one of the ten we carry. This afternoon I was at Action Stations with them all and we did a close-down gas exercise. The screen doors were closed as well as all the scuttles, and all the ventilation was off below. Before long, up came an ML motor launch, something like an MTB, and dropped tear-gas canisters. This meant that we had to wear our respirators for an hour. You got used to this but it was not so good for those who were sporting a beard!

That night we should have been anchored at Marshollot Bay but instead we dropped the hook outside the harbour. We were due to sail for Algiers at 11.45 p.m. in company with *Delight* and *Birmingham*. We knew that we would be doing an exercise of one sort or another with them. I had decided not to go ashore at Algiers so as to save as much as possible for Pauline's visit. That night I did a final baking for some time. The D.O. had decided to buy bread from Algiers. It was terrible stuff, as I remember – something like French bread but very coarse.

On the voyage we spent the time tearing round the ocean. The fuel we were using must have been terrific. One morning we had a shoot at a sleeve target. X Turret blew the sleeve clean out of the sky and for that received a commendation.

We were due back in Malta only two days before Pauline's arrival. The D.O. asked me whether she was still coming and I assured him that she was. That meant that he would not have forgotten to arrange for my leave. I was the only one in our branch whose wife was coming out, which made it all the easier for me to be spared. The others were taking weekend leave.

While I was baking at 12 o'clock that night, the D.O. came to see me. He wanted me to put in a request for a week's leave from the 21st October, which I did the next day, having heard from Pauline that she was definitely coming. When I read Orders for the following day, I saw that libertymen were warned to go in threes – a sure sign of political trouble in the offing.

We were warned to 'keep out of Casbar' and all the old routine. I got a letter to say that Pauline was coming for two weeks. Then that got stretched to a far longer period, and all in all we both had a lovely time – this even though I had had only two days to get a flat and get it equipped. On looking back, I believe we borrowed some gear from the ship.

CHAPTER VII

The Second Half of the Mediterranean Tour

By now it was early January, 1956. We had given up our flat, where we had had such a happy time, and I tidied up and returned the keys. The quite generous allotment of leave which I had been given in Malta was, I believe, largely due to the Chief Cook, good old Monty Banks. I very nearly missed Pauline's plane home, I remember, because I thought she would be held up in customs far longer than she was.

The next day we came out of drydock. The day after that the First Lord of The Admiralty came to give us a talk on H.M.S. *Birmingham* and a hundred men from each ship had to be present for it.

That was on a Friday and on the Saturday we left harbour and set out on an all-night cruise to see if everything was working satisfactorily after our refit.

After a further week in harbour, we were to go to sea to take part in more exercises and then, we believed, to pay a visit to a Spanish port.

Our Captain certainly didn't waste time! Soon after leaving harbour we exercised 'Fire on B Gun Deck', sent the boat away to recover a lifebelt that had been thrown over the side and also exercised 'Collision Stations'.

By this time I was baking on my own each night and finding it much better; I knew where I stood. I used to start my first dough at 5 p.m. and by the time I had finished all my work, it would be 5 a.m. Then I would sleep all morning and perhaps start again at 5 p.m. the next evening. However, I used to keep this up for only six days at a time. We also used to get bread from the Army at Famagusta in Cyprus, but when we could not, we had, of course, to bake it ourselves and that fell to me. In addition, Captain's Rounds was looming near and the Chief Cook wanted the galley thoroughly cleaned and smartened up, which would include painting, polishing and scrubbing. As there was to be no Admiral's Inspection, the Captain's Rounds were to be a substitute for it and, with a Captain like ours, far more thorough and severe. All in all I was working flat out and fell to wondering why they did not call me 'Dobbin', 'Prince', or some other horse name – especially as I was short-handed, Mick having burnt himself badly with a bowl of hot fat.

We were on the lookout for gun-runners but had had no excitement so far. Then one night we found ourselves steaming at 20 knots for the north of the island, where apparently we had had an anonymous tip-off that there might be an attempt to land arms. You could always tell when the ship was moving at speed, even when below. You could feel the power and she used to bounce slightly. We found a yacht one night but she was outside the three-mile limit so we were unable to board her. She was also flying the American flag, though this might have been a blind. In the end we circled her and let her go.

Soon after this we headed for the coast of Israel and joined in the Levant Patrol. Our programme was to take us to Port Said by the 27th and we were due to arrive back in Malta on the 13th and Gibraltar on 18th. Then we would be going home, arriving in Chatham on the 26th March. According to the D.O., I could then be spared to do my P.O.'s Course, since we would be in Chatham for some time during the summer. We would be sailing with the Home Fleet at the beginning of May. I asked Pauline to book us both into the NAAFI Club.

We were also due to escort the *Britannia* for the Queen's State Visit to Stockholm in June. For this we were to have saluting guns put in place. On the day we had Captain's Rounds, he said he was very pleased with the state of both galleys and with the ship generally, though it was a heck of a job to keep up such high standards. We were due in to Port Said the following day. By this time we were buying bread from the Egyptians but the D.O. was trying to keep it to a minimum. That meant that I still had to do a lot of baking. One compensation was that we could get excellent fruit there, especially bananas, which I loved. We stayed the night at Port Said and then returned to Famagusta, where we hoped to pick up some mail. We were due to remain on the Cyprus Patrol for a further week before dropping down into Haifa for four days and then returning to Malta. So by the 15th, we hoped, our bows would be pointing home. At Famagusta we were able to get really good lettuce, spring onions and tomatoes, and we could make excellent salads, which certainly made a change. The grapefruit, oranges, bananas and tangerines were equally good and cheap. Those were the days! Since then the best fruit and vegetables have all gone for export. We estimated that it would take two days from Malta to Gibraltar and then six from there to home. We thought that the last bit was rather long until we found that we would be taking part in an exercise with the Home Fleet named 'Grey Dawn'.

Already by this time we were hearing rumours of where we would be going after joining the Home Fleet, namely Invergordon and Londonderry. On the way to Famagusta we ran into yet another gale but fortunately it was relatively short-lived. We managed to get some bread from a supply ship, the *Fort Duquesne*, but less than I had hoped, which meant that I would be baking again the following night.

We left Famagusta at 3 p.m. and spent the rest of the day on patrol before anchoring that night at Karovastatsi.

One day the D.O. came and asked me whether I would be signing on for a further period of service and I replied that I would not (Little did I know then!). He suggested that I should go and have a talk with him some time. As already mentioned, I had been unable to attend the Cookery School in Malta and I wasn't sure whether I would get another opportunity to do my P.O.'s Course, or even if I did and passed, whether I would have time to pick up my rate.

On the *Defender*, I should explain, baking always caused problems. We could never do enough, which meant that it had to be rationed to the various messes. This caused some difficulty. I had to store the bread in lockers in the Canteen Flat. The doors were locked but certain members of the crew used to force the corners of the locker down and steal bread from them.

The following day we were due to fire Squids and some of the guns, just to check them for accuracy. We also did some speed trials and managed to get up to 42 knots, which we considered pretty good. Everything had now been checked and was in running order except for one of the evaporators used to make fresh water. The previous day's speed trials had caused it to 'go bust'. As a result, we were forced to economise in our use of fresh water for a while.

One morning a telegram arrived for the butcher saying that his mother had passed away. Within an hour he had been granted home leave from the C.-in-C.'s Office, and it was arranged for him to fly home next day. If anything of that sort happened, the Navy used to take every possible step to rush leave through for the individual concerned. The butcher arrived home only fifteen hours after the news had been broken to him.

A few days later I saw my Service Certificate, which we were shown every six months. In February I got a 'V.G.', again in April, and then 'Satisfactory' down to the last five months. Then the D.O. gave me a 'Superior'. If I did decide to go through for P.O., this would certainly help.

I heard some of us would be going ashore at Karovastatsi as guests of the Army, and that we would also be having a number of soldiers from the Highland Light Infantry on board in exchange. Really it was a good-will trip and we sometimes did have exchanges of this kind between the Services.

I had to bake again on both Saturday and Sunday night, since we had been unable to get any bread from other sources. We did one more gun-running patrol on Sunday night and then sailed for Haifa, where we arrived the following morning. There were Rounds again – they never seemed to let up. Sometimes it was the Skipper's, sometimes Jimmy the One's. I was hoping that Customs would be kind to us. They always used to do the officers first and then the P.O.'s, where there would be plenty of rum, so that by the time they got to us they would have had quite a bit. (This time, however, I got caned.)

By now we were already steaming along the coast of Cyprus and had reached a place called Daylors. In some of these regions the scenery was quite magnificent – hills something like the Irish or Scottish hills, not barren as those in the Middle East so often are. We could see some quite modern buildings gleaming white in the sunshine. What a pity that there was so much political unrest. Greece seemed to be deliberately stirring it up and of course the religious leaders were at it too.

From the delightful bay where we were anchored we could see all the tents of the Army encampment. We now had about twenty soldiers on board, two of them being in our mess. They were to come to sea with us that night and in the morning we were due to drop them off before going on to Famagusta for some mail. After that we would be doing a patrol and then on course for Haifa.

I did wish that the authorities would make their minds up as to where our bread was coming from. I was told that I would not have to bake that night or the next, which could only mean that it was being obtained from the Army or the *Fort Duquesne*, the supply ship. The soldiers were lying on their bunks, not actually seasick but finding the movement of the ship strange, and of course the stuffiness below didn't help. Those damn buzzes that kept going round the ship! The latest was that we would be doing an extra Levant Patrol, which would mean that we wouldn't be home until the 1st April. Smudge, the Boy Seaman, went up to the Captain's cabin to find out unofficially. Then one of the Seamen heard the First Lieutenant telling the officers in the wardroom that the soldiers would be staying on board a few days longer – another change of plan! We had a Cypriot policeman on board in case we picked up a gun-runner. His role would be to act as interpreter.

A day or so later the Captain Cleared Lower Deck and told us one or two things. We were to arrive at Sheerness at 8 a.m. on the 26th and would be in the lock at Chatham by 9 a.m. We would have to wait for the tide. The Captain also spoke about Haifa. It seemed that an Arab-Jewish war was all but inevitable. Hostilities might break out any time, but probably either that month or the next. Those going ashore at Haifa, therefore, had to watch themselves so as to avoid starting anything off. We ought to think ourselves lucky on our little island that we have so little unrest. The Captain was quite good at giving any information he had on future movements. He gave us dates and places for our summer cruise, though these, he said, were subject to probable changes. We were definitely to leave Chatham on 30th April, and would be arriving at Portland on 31st. From there we were to leave on either 1st or 2nd May and arrive at Brest on the 4th. After that we were to sail for Invergordon on the 8th, arriving on the 13th. We would be leaving Invergordon on the 13th and arriving at Portsmouth on the 31st. We would remain there five days, leaving on the 31st June. Then on to Middlesborough, but the dates were uncertain. We would arrive at Stockholm with the Queen on *Britannia* on 8th June, and leave on the 18th. Then on to Kiel on 20th and leaving on the 24th, arriving at Copenhagen on the 26th and leaving on the 2nd July. Then we would be going on an exercise and so to Rosyth, arriving on 6th and leaving for Dover on 13th July. (In the event we brought the King of Iraq from Ostend to Dover as he hated flying.) We would be leaving Dover on 16th and arriving at Margate on 17th and Chatham on 23rd July. Once there, so I was told, we would be doing a self-maintenance re-fit and it was then that I hoped to have the chance to do my P.O.'s Course. (In the event my hopes were dashed, because by that time we had film people on board.)

The Highland Light Infantry soldiers left us at Famagusta as bad weather was forecast. If it had become rough, we would have had a bit of a job to get them off, as we would have been unable either to lower boats or to go alongside anywhere. We were due in off Haifa on the Tuesday following, and the Jews would probably view unfavourably the presence of any British soldiers on board. The soldiers would not have liked it either. The D.O. asked me again whether I would be signing on and again I told him that I would not. What I didn't know at the time was that if I wanted to sign on after 21st March, it would have to be for another five years. By the time I was finished on the *Defender*, I would have been at sea for four years: one year on *Solebay*, one and a half on *Barcarole*, and one and a half on *Defender*. (I mustn't forget the *Calton*, where I had only six weeks to do.)

We had returned to Famagusta amid gale conditions, which fortunately soon blew themselves out. By midnight it had become quite calm.

We arrived at Haifa at 8 a.m. The two ships who were to be relieved were the *Undean* and the *Ursa*. They would be going to take our place in Cyprus, which meant that we had definitely finished there. At Haifa our arrival seemed to cause quite a stir and once we came alongside, a barrier had to be put round the gangway and an Army and Police Guard mounted. We also had our own sentry on the jetty. The Army and Navy all used to carry arms.

Soon after we were secured, we could see a party – including women – carrying out rifle drill just opposite to us. Nazareth wasn't very far away – only about 40 kilometres – and the Navy had laid on a coach trip there for the following day. I was hoping to go as I had always wanted to visit one of the major holy places. Meanwhile the Captain had granted shore leave for all those not on duty.

The Chief Cook seemed to think that Pauline and I were made of money. 'Bring Pauline down to Chatham for a fortnight,' he airily suggested. 'and you can both stay at the NAAFI Club!'

The D.O. again asked me whether I was going to sign on for further service and again I told him 'No'. Mick did sign on. My impression was that Haifa had a good-sized harbour. The town was built on the side of a mountain and the buildings were square and tall.

Another coach trip had been laid on, this time to an oil refinery. I put my name down, but rather late, and was very doubtful whether there would be room for me.

We arrived back from Nazareth about 2 p.m. What a smashing morning we had spent! It was a thoroughly excellent tour, full of historical interest. We set off from the ship at 7.55 a.m. in two well-equipped and comfortable coaches carrying 40 passengers each. The driver spoke English and acted as one of our two guides, the other being an Israeli officer whose English was excellent. We went through Haifa and climbed Mount Carmel, which is on the inland side of the town. The road up the mountain was very windy and steep and the view of the town and harbour from the top was quite striking. Then we went on to a Cathedral with a gold-plated dome, belonging to one or other of the Christian sects here. Anyone, of any religion, was allowed to pray there, so long as he believed in one God. The Cathedral was not open but the gardens surrounding it were beautiful. After circling the top of Carmel, we set off for Nazareth itself, with various stops along the way – for instance, the Valley of Armageddon, where the final battle with the forces of evil is, I believe, destined to be fought. We also saw the valley where David slew Goliath. The route to Nazareth took us up and down over hills and valleys, which were well cultivated and thick with vegetation. This surprised me; I had always thought the Holy Land was largely desert, which was certainly not the case here. Most of the people in Haifa were wearing European clothes, but out in the countryside many were in Arab dress. We even saw an encampment of nomads. When we arrived at Nazareth, we had a bottle of pop at a hotel and bought a few cards and two mother-of-pearl rosaries. Another guide, this time an Arab, undertook to show us round. Nazareth seemed quite small, consisting of not much more than a main road and a small crossroads. The people gave the impression of being very much the same as they must have been 2,000 years ago. The women were carrying pitchers on their heads and many of the men were riding donkeys. It can't have changed that much since Our Lord lived there. Next the guide took us up a slight hill to a kind of building site where a Cathedral building was planned. It was to be bigger than the Vatican Basilica and was on the site of a church which had been pulled down and re-built more than once. Right in the middle of all the rubble was a door and steps leading down to a cave beneath. Here, we were told, Mary and Joseph lived, as well as Jesus himself for 27 years, and the Angel Gabriel appeared to them. It was pretty small: a main cave with alcoves leading off. In the main cave stood a very impressive altar. After returning up the steps, we walked on and a little further came to a monastery which had been built in 1930 on the site of the carpenter's shop. At the centre of the church and to the left was a V-shaped flight of steps which were steep and narrow enough to make it awkward to get down them, especially as the ceiling was very low. (I believe it was closed a few years after we had visited it.) Directly beneath was another cave, also with alcoves leading off, though these were barred and grilled. Probably they were used as sleeping quarters or even as stables for the animals and perhaps it was only relatively recently that it had been decided to preserve them as far as possible in their original state. The ceiling was very high and dome-shaped and here and there you could actually see the marks of the tools which had been used to carve it out. It was black from the oil of lamps used for cooking and lighting. The main room was almost circular in shape and shelves had been cut into the rock. There was also a narrow well, with a piece of rock removed to allow for a rope to be let down. This was thin and worn, not from rubbing against the rock but from constant handling. At the centre of the cave stood what looked like a round table about waist high. When I asked the guide about it, he replied: 'That's no table, that's the original floor!' We could understand, therefore, why it had to be closed off.

We returned to the bus, bought some oranges, and then headed back for Haifa. About halfway on the journey back we called at a kibbutz where the inhabitants – all Jews, though from 29 different countries – were completely self-sufficient. They had their own school, living quarters and dining-room, where we were invited to have a meal. However, we had to decline because of lack of time and having so much to see. The kibbutz was government-controlled and the people had to labour in the fields with armed guards to protect them from the Arabs, who used to attack them and destroy their crops. There were 150 adults and 200 children. They didn't get any pay; and profits from the produce they grew went towards the communal expenses and the modernisation of the kibbutz.

The next night I did manage to get in that trip to the oil refinery after all. When we arrived, we were shown into a big hall, and that was about all we saw of the place. All those who worked there were English and the directors and bosses of the refinery had organised a major party for us. Their wives were there as well. What a party we had and all so unexpected! Performers and dancers stood on tables and we were given crisps, sandwiches with peanut butter and just about all the 'big eats' you could think of. We had a good singsong, there were stacks of beer, and they never left us with an empty glass. About midnight the buses which they had laid on to fetch and carry us took us back to the ship, and we felt dumbfounded by the hospitality we had received. We had expected to be shown the workings of the refinery itself. As it was, in the true naval tradition, this was classed as a 'good run ashore'.

The next night and the night after that the Wardroom was holding two cocktail parties. In addition the ship was going to be open to visitors. Here all the women from the age of 18 used to do National Service together with the men. It was strange. Here we were in a country apparently on the verge of war, and yet the atmosphere seemed so relaxed and joyful. Martial law was already in force and all members of the armed forces were armed. Throughout the town ack-ack machine gun emplacements, surrounded with barbed wire, were already in place on the flat roofs. What was unmistakably clear, though, was that they liked us here, ours being the first British ship to have visited Haifa in the past three years. During our visit the Commander of the Israeli Navy came aboard. We had a great welcome from all the population. We played football, basketball and table tennis matches against teams from among the people of Haifa and enjoyed numerous free trips. There was to be another trip to Nazareth next day and a trip had also been arranged to another biblical site, namely Accra. In addition, a visit to a glass factory had been laid on. We were open again to visitors but the police had limited visitors only to those holding special passes.

At last we were on our way back to Malta, with every turn of the screws taking us nearer home. We would not be getting any further mail until we reached Malta itself. We were due in early a few mornings later. We would be leaving for Gibraltar on the Thursday and then meeting up with the Home Fleet.

I was baking again the night after we left Haifa. The D.O. did not like the idea of buying Israeli bread. I never used to mind working on my own at night. It made a change from daytime work in the galley. At night the galley used to look a whole lot better – to me at least. For instance all my laundry would be hanging up. Also, about 1 a.m., I used to cook myself a very large pork chop.

When we got to Gibraltar, we expected to find 49 ships already in harbour. It was also expected that the last lap of our voyage around the Bay of Biscay would be rough, as it usually was at that time of year. We would not be going through the Bay itself but giving it a wide berth, but even so we had to be ready for the worst. We expected to be arriving in the lock at Chatham about 11.10. It was better in a way, since there might be a chance of getting through Customs before Pauline came aboard. If that failed to materialize, we could be in for a long wait, since no leave would be granted until Customs had cleared us. We would probably be in the Basin, perhaps tying up in the berth where the *Superb* had been.

At Malta I received a bumper mail, which took me from 12.30 to 2.30 to read. When I told the Chief what a lot of letters I had received, he replied: 'Well, you had better answer them this afternoon'! He should have said 'in the next few days'. When we arrived in Grand Harbour, we found our sister ships, *Daring* and *Duchess*, already there. However, we hadn't seen our heavenly twin, the *Delight*, since we left Gibraltar. We were secured to our old billet, opposite Senglea. I haggled with a Maltese trader for an embroidered table runner, beating the price down by more than ten shillings. I also bought a few more presents for members of the family.

Two Officers' Cooks came on board at Malta, which would certainly ease the strain on the rest of us since it doubled the staff. By this time we were proceeding nice and steady at cruising speed. I was to have little more baking to do – no more than a couple of nights – so for the most part I would be doing day work.

When we arrived at Gib. I was astonished at the number of ships – I had never seen so many at once, foreign as well as English, and the Destroyer pens all full. The *Ark* and *Birmingham* were there and also an Australian Carrier, the *Melbourne*. I couldn't see any sign of the Royal Yacht but expected to see her soon. We were due to do an exercise with her in the Home Fleet. We moved into the harbour and secured alongside, but the swell and wind were so strong that we had to move outside again and drop anchor, and it was decided that we should remain there until our departure on Tuesday morning.

The rest of the voyage was fairly uneventful. We left Chatham at 3 p.m. and arrived at Sheerness around 5.15. Leave started at 6 p.m. and I was on duty watch with a lot of cleaning to do as well as the cooking. I heard that some ready-furnished Navy flats were to be had at Chatham and that all you had to do was apply for one, so I decided to do so as soon as possible. We might probably have to wait some time before a flat became available. We left for Portland and put to sea again almost immediately. We did one exercise on the way in order to test the equipment. We arrived at Invergordon on the same day and were due to leave on 31st June. Portsmouth had by this time been eliminated from the programme. We would be leaving Dover on the 18th July and arriving at Margate on 19th.

At 5.15 one evening we held the ceremony of Sprinkling the Ashes at Sea. We had a Padre on board from the *Delight*. I believe that the dead person was a friend or relative of the Captain's.

I could not yet put in my application for a flat since the Ship's Office were too much occupied with doing the pay ledgers.I duly put in my application the next day. We arrived at Portland, fuelled and left immediately for Brest, making our way there at a steady cruising speed. As we drew near, we ran into some quite thick fog. Brest seemed to be quite a large Naval Base, rather on the same scale as Chatham. Every other day I was rising at 4 a.m. and the following day I was on duty from 8 a.m. to 8 p.m. and from 4 to 12 the next morning.

We had Captain's Rounds again, which meant even more cleaning up than usual in the galley. The workmen stripped down the deckhead over the top of the range and copper and left a lot of rubbish after they had put it all back again.

The *Tyne* was with us along with the *Delight*, and it seemed that the three ships would have a relatively easy time of it, with only three days of exercising out of about 20 days of sea time.

A lot of men had been coming back from runs ashore in a terrible state and this was attributed to mixing beer with the local wine. In the course of his leave, Love the cook patched things up with his wife and later went ashore on a date. I used to find his morals hateful and also the way he kept trying to get out of work and was always borrowing. On the anniversary of VE Day we dressed ship and all the sailors on board had the afternoon off. I believe the French did the same. We opened the ship to visitors all afternoon and many came to visit us.

A diesel motor broke down one day and we were forced to lay on a cold lunch. However, it was repaired within a few hours, and to make up we gave the crew a supper of roast veal, cauliflower, stuffing, roast potatoes followed by prunes and custard.

We left for Invergordon at 10 a.m. and soon found ourselves working our way through the Irish Sea up the west coast of Scotland in rather rough weather. The wind was Force 8. As we passed through the Western Isles, we looked very smart with seven ships in line, and before long we were passing through Scapa Flow. Though the weather was still rough, thank goodness, we had a stern sea, which made it not quite so bad.

One morning as we were oiling, the pipe broke with the result that our side was covered with oil. We got in to Invergordon about 4.30 p.m. There had been quite a bit of trouble on board lately with too many coming back adrift, and now the Captain had announced that he was to grant privileged leave only in Stockholm and Copenhagen. That meant that any lads who had come back late over the last six months couldn't go ashore. We hoped we would be leaving Invergordon and going on to Rosyth.

The following Wednesday I was roped in for a Landing Party skylark and we went ashore with full equipment for some type of exercise. We landed about 9.30 and arrived back at 3.15 p.m. By this time more buzzes were flying around. The ship was to be stripped and re-painted in a lighter grey. Due to the continuing rough weather, we thought we might be moving to Rosyth after all, since there was more shelter there. The wind was so strong that no boats were going between ships or landing liberty men. Some Norwegian ships arrived for some major exercise that was due to start the following week. We would be missing it, however. All the Seamen were doing in the rough weather was to lower and raise the boats. Eventually the wind abated enough for quite a few to go ashore, but if the wind picked up again they would have to spend the night on the *Glasgow*.

A few days later we seemed to be doing just about everything: firing torpedoes and recovering them, firing off all the big guns and all the smaller armament as well. In addition to all these exercises, we were scheduled to do a Night Encounter but at the last minute it was cancelled. After all that we found that we would be doing no more exercises of that kind for the time being, since all we would be firing from then on would be the Saluting Guns.

CHAPTER VIII

Royal State Visits

IT WAS ABOUT THIS TIME that we started getting ready to meet the Royal Yacht at Middlesborough. At this stage I was still in the after galley while Mick was in the forrard one. When the Chief took Lynn away too, we were busier than ever, especially as few went ashore for the weekend. I myself had a brief run ashore in Invergordon and found the poverty and the number of derelict houses rather depressing. Sunday was particularly bleak up there with absolutely nothing to do, both pubs and cinema being closed. This was Scotland! However I did manage to buy Pauline a small doll in Highland dress, something I had been planning to do while at sea.

It was Captain's Rounds again and he said how pleased he was with my galley. He told me to keep up the high standard I had achieved. I should think so too, considering the amount of work I put into it!

On Whitsunday we had a service on board and I went to Divisions on the forecastle. While I was on parade, blow me if a damn great seagull didn't come and strike my arm a glancing blow and then make a mess right down my arm and all down the leg of my trousers! I had to go and get it washed off.

After Divisions the Captain told us that the First Sea Lord, Admiral Lord Louie Mountbatten, would be coming round. He would go wherever he liked. The after galley was a showpiece and the Captain always used to treat it as such, whereas the other ships didn't bother. So I hoped he would come to see me. After the Captain had finished speaking to everyone, he dismissed Divisions but told all Leading Rates to stand fast. He then said that out of 57 leave-breakers, 11 were Leading Hands and that it had got to stop. We had to set an example.

We had a few nicknames for the Captain. If he turned the ship sharply while at sea, we called him 'Good Old Hard Over'. Another name for him was 'Lord Head', but he was most often known to us as 'Father' or 'Dad'. He would be the senior Captain of the escort group, so I pitied the *Delight* and the new Canadian Destroyer which was to join the escort.

We left Invergordon on the 1st June and the next part of the programme was designed to give us a chance to get on with the painting that needed to be done. We would be at or near Middlesborough and then of course the ceremonies would be starting.

One morning I lent an AB a broom to sweep down X Gun Deck and he must have been throwing it around or something, because it went over the side. The Officer of the Watch saw it go, told him to report to me, and said that I had to take the necessary action.

So we went in front of the Officer of the Watch. The upshot was that he was on First Lieutenant's Defaulters the next morning. He would probably have to pay for the broom and in addition get three or four days 10A, which meant stoppage of leave and tot, as well as extra work morning and night, since it was lost through negligence. Two leading E.A.'s and one O.E. joined us and were assigned to a mess made up of miscellaneous Leading Hands, including the two Leading Stores Hands, Mick, Derby and myself.

One day the powers that be decided to hold an obstacle race for whalers from all ships. It involved rowing half a mile, sailing half a mile, rowing half a mile. Our ship won and received a cup to prove it.

A Dutch Cruiser came in one day while we were still at Invergordon. They would all be going to sea at some time in the very near future (perhaps next day), and I found myself wishing that we were joining them. It was becoming so boring just hanging about.

A day or two later we had a 'Custard Bosun', i.e. a Warrant Cookery Officer, probably the Fleet's, on board. He was quite pleased with everything but they never used to say much.

Lord Louie came on board a few mornings later and spoke to the ship's company, but at the time I was busy in the galley. I saw him leave in a boat after 15 minutes, so he didn't manage his walkabout after all. His programme was too tight.

All this time we were still painting ship, but soon after Lord Louie's visit the Fleet sailed, all except for the *Tyne* and the *Delight*. Soon after this the Captain looked in and asked whether everything was all right. He told me that the First Sea Lord was sorry to have been unable to come around. I told him everything had been ready and he replied 'I'm sure it was,' and with those words, left.

The O.A's and E.A.'s had now been aboard for about a week and they were staying. Our Mess was down to the level it was at before. I was sleeping in a hammock and unfortunately had had to put up with a medium-sized one; there were no long ones available. That was the trouble with hammocks; they were too short. I used not to mind sleeping in one but preferred a bunk as it was longer.

I liked this Mess far more than the one I had been in because no one caused any trouble. In 11 Mess there was always a P.O. shouting at someone. Then, of course, there were nineteen in it whereas down here we were only nine.

A few days later we had Senior Supply Officer's Rounds. It meant being inspected by a Captain from the Flag Ship. I was unable to use the after galley that day because a dynamo generator stopped and the supply of electricity was insufficient. The Senior Supply Officer duly inspected us and was quite pleased with everything. He asked me what Engagement I was on and when I told him I was due to finish in April, he asked whether I was married, what work I would be doing and where I was going to live. He was really nosey, but in a pleasant sort of way.

I had a little note handed to me from a Quartermaster. It said: 'To Joe from the Middle Watchmen. It's sung to the tune of 'Davey Crockett':

Down in the galley, frying sailors' fish,
When Joe is finished, it's fit for any dish.
He could cook when he was only three,
Now he's the Leading C.

I had never been to Middlesborough or Hartlepool. The day after we arrived was the Queen's Birthday and we had Divisions and fired a 21-Gun Salute. To my disappointment, my new cap had not arrived as it should have done, and I would certainly be needing it for Stockholm. I knew I would have to chase the tailors up. We anchored about two miles off shore and the conditions were too rough for us to lower a boat. The weekenders and libertymen were decidedly fed up – especially Derby, who had to bake that night instead of going ashore. After the State Visit to Stockholm we believed that we would be going to Chatham for six weeks and then to Invergordon to have the guns taken off. Then on to Hamburg.

While we were waiting off Middlesborough, we fired another Salute and also manned the side, as we would be doing at Stockholm. All the Ship's Company stood in line at the rail and when the order 'caps off' was given, you would cheer and at the same time you would move the cap you were holding in your hand in an anti-clockwise direction. Whether I would get my new cap in time was now questionable.

A few nights later, with still no leave being given, Derby had to make three doughs. Then, just as he had finished, a boat arrived with the bread from ashore. He had to finish his baking, of course, but was he fed up!

The next day leave was given and only the messman and myself were left on board in No. 5 – it was so quiet and pleasant. The following day we left and had our rendezvous with the Royal Yacht on the Tuesday morning. We were due to fire a number of Salutes. The trouble for me was that the Saluting Guns were positioned directly above my galley, which made the noise deafening and the vibrations potentially damaging.

On our arrival in Stockholm, the King of Sweden would be meeting us accompanied by two Cruisers, a number of Destroyers and M.T.B.'s, as well as contingents from the Swedish Air Force. Then we would all be going up river to the city itself, and more Salutes were due to be fired there.

Most of the libertymen returned, but what a tale there was to tell! Derby and a Seaman were in jail on about a dozen charges, the main one being breaking and entering. So that was his stand-over gone. The D.O. and the Padre were trying to get them back. Most of the stories were of a similar kind. One chap was thoroughly drunk and a girl took him to her home, where the family tried to sober him up, but he flaked out on the settee. He woke up at about 4 a.m. and found himself halfway up the stairs. He shouted: 'Hey, I've got to get back – where am I?' About twenty of the libertymen could find nowhere to sleep, so they climbed aboard a tug and when they woke up, they found themselves at sea! In the end, however, they all got safely back to the ship, although that morning there were certainly some thick heads!

A night or two later we joined up with the Canadian ship, the *St. Laurent*, and the *Delight* was also with us. We waited for *Britannia* at the mouth of the Tees and all fired a 21-Gun Salute. The Yacht passed us and took the lead with us on the starboard side, *Delight* on the port and the *St. Laurent* in the centre astern. I was looking through the scuttle when the Yacht passed by but did not see the Queen. However, even without that, the sight of all three ships in line abreast firing Salutes with aircraft above was a truly impressive one.

Derby came back at last. They had bailed him out but he would have to return to court on 27th July. The D.O. defended him. We were now dressed overall, with a line of flags from the bows to the mast, from there to the second and smaller mast, and so down to the stern. We had already flown them on the Queen's birthday and were now doing so again. The only time the Jack was flown at sea nowadays was when acting as escort.

We were still maintaining the same course and formation, but now altering course slightly to turn for Sweden. The weather was a bit rough but not bad enough to necessitate any alteration to the programme and the *Britannia* was fitted with stabilisers. Just as well, since the Queen was reputed to be a poor sailor. The very next day it blew up to a gale, and that night we drew apart so as to safeguard the ships against the danger of a collision. We then altered our formation to 'In Line Ahead' with *Britannia* in the lead, followed by *Defender*, *Delight* and H.M.C.S. *St. Laurent* in that order. We passed through the Kattegat and later through the Sound, a narrow passage between Sweden on one side and the Danish islands and Copenhagen on the other. Two Danish Destroyers came close to us and fired a Salute. Then as we drew near to land – whether Norway or Sweden I am not sure – a great number of small craft came out to us and followed us for some time. Two hours later we came close to the Swedish coast, where quite a large armada was waiting for us. Small ketches, launches, boats etc. came quite close, waving and shouting 'Welcome to Sweden!'. After a time these too fell back and I think most of them must have come from Gothenburg.

In the closing stages of this trip the question of my drafting came up again. I declined to put in for the P.O.'s course. What would be the point since I was refusing a recommissioning? I had to fill in a form stating three places I would like to go, so I put Chatham, *Ganges*, and the Air Station, Ford at Arundel.

By this time we were encountering patches of fog all day, which caused us to break the line of formation. Since leaving England a terrific amount of cleaning and painting work had been done. The Upper Deck was painted green and black.

The next day the King of Sweden joined us and we exchanged Salutes between his ship and ours. It all started at 5.30 a.m. We entered the river early and picked up two pilots for each ship. By that time, however, the fog was so bad that we had to wait until after 9.30 before we moved off. The *Britannia* had already gone ahead, and it started to rain intermittently. Then the sun came out and we had to belt along at 24 knots to catch up with the Royal Yacht. There was a great number of islands at the mouth of the river and as we passed close to them, we could see huge crowds of people waving. The river itself was quite long and it took us a good three hours to make our way upstream to the city itself. As we entered the river, four Swedish M.T.B.'s came tearing past us. They had missed the Royal Yacht in the fog and could they move! On the way up we met hundreds of smaller vessels of all sizes and descriptions: yachts, launches, motor boats etc. Still steaming like mad, we fired a Salute to Sweden. A castle came into view and the shore battery exchanged Salutes with us. People were shouting 'Welcome to Sweden!' and waving flags. What a spectacle it was! Even then we had not yet caught up with the Royal Yacht. Then jet fighters from the Swedish Air Force flew over us and by 11.30 we had at last caught up with *Britannia*. More Salutes followed and when when we finally got in, the crowds on the roof tops and at the windows were almost unbelievable. All the traffic had stopped. The Royal Yacht anchored and we ourselves secured with the *St. Laurent* on our starboard side and the *Delight* alongside the wall. The Queen went ashore in the State Launch and we fired our last Salute.

Stockholm itself struck me as marvellously beautiful. I was able to get ashore and the warmth of the welcome we received was almost indescribable. People were coming up to us and shaking our hands in the streets, offering us drinks and inviting us to their homes. 'Welcome to Sweden,' they were shouting, 'Long live the Queen of England!' English was their second language, so on the whole there was no real barrier between us. One man who invited me to have a meal and even to stay at his home was so cordial that I began to have my suspicions as to his motives. But I was ashamed of them later. He was just a deeply kind and hospitable man with a great liking for the English. I thoroughly enjoyed his company and seeing his home and family.

After we had fired our final Salute to the Queen, we moved further in and secured behind the *Delight*, with the Royal Yacht opposite to us and the *St. Laurent* behind us.

The Queen came aboard us on Monday at 10.30 and had photographs taken on the forecastle. It was only a brief visit, however, because her schedule was so tight and she was visiting the other two escort ships as well. During the visit I was working in the galley, but I did see her from a distance. She was quite small and the Duke of Edinburgh seemed to tower over her. Everything went very well, though she didn't come to visit the galley as I had hoped. That day she spliced the mainbrace, which was very welcome and meant that we had an extra tot.

The Captain was very pleased with the ship both inside and out. My galley in particular was gleaming and polished, but what a job it was to keep those high standards up!

The lads – including, I am sorry to say, the married ones – were going out with various girls. Lynn, the cook who had recently got married to a Scottish girl, was one of the culprits. I told him that the ink was hardly dry on his marriage certificate and that he ought to be ashamed of himself.

The *St. Laurent* left at 3 a.m. and the *Britannia* was the next to go, with ourselves and the *Delight* leaving the next day bound for Kiel. After Kiel we separated, with *Delight* going to Norway and ourselves to Copenhagen. Following upon the Royal Visit, the Queen sent a signal, published in Daily Orders, saying how pleased she had been with her Darings and wishing us luck. There was also an article in the *Evening Standard* saying how smart *Defender* was etc. I should think so too, considering the officers we had to ensure that she was kept that way! The Captain had no complaints and was very pleased and we had no trouble from anyone on board during the ten-days' stay.

We duly arrived at Kiel, but though shore leave was given, not many took advantage of it and I got the impression that the ship's company did not like

Best pipe of the day – Up Spirits!

it much. Certainly I did not. The few who did go ashore came back saying that it was 'punk of duff', another Naval expression which I taught Pauline. An ex-German Admiral came on board. He was quite an old man, dressed, of course, in civilian clothes, and was given a 13-gun Salute. The same French Cruiser that was at Brest was here too, and also two American Destroyers.

We were getting bread from the shore and it was of the German kind – a horrible dark brown. We held a party for English children which was a great success and they obviously enjoyed themselves. The next day the ship was open to visitors, so I closed the galley for the period of the visit. Having them all staring at you as you were working was like being an animal in the zoo.

Later I did go on a trip which had been organised to two large villages called Pleetz and Ploon. There were 20 of us, 20 from the *Delight*, and 20 from the German Navy. We had just started to give the Germans some ships and so far they had had two coastal minesweepers and a larger vessel. They had only 500 in their Navy. Their uniforms were the same as during the War, except that now they had our type of collars. We had a look at Pleetz and Ploon and had coffee and cakes at Ploon. The countryside was pleasant enough, with lakes and forests, but we kept our reserve with the Germans and all sat separately. By the time we got back to Pleetz, a few of us had broken the ice to some extent with the Germans and in the end got on quite well with them. Later we gave some of them tea on the *Defender* and a tour of the ship, which they greatly enjoyed. One or two spoke English which made things easier.

The Fleet Cookery Officer came on board and stayed with us until we reached Chatham. He was a nice chap who asked me why I didn't sign on again. The Senior Cookery Officer who came to see us at *Tyne* had sent in a highly favourable report on us to the Admiralty. Apparently it was quite a 'Recommend', and he said that we were the cleanest Daring he had been on and he had seen all of them. Unlike the *Delight*, we have avoided painting over our brightwork and have kept it all polished and shining.

One day we had a bit of fun. A German Commie was on the jetty and he was running us down. Someone turned a hose on him and later the Police arrested him.

We left Kiel at 11.30 on the 26th June bound for Copenhagen. On our last night at Kiel we had a thoroughly good time. We were invited to dinner on a German ship and beer and brandy were being drunk. The German Captain himself (the equivalent of a Lieutenant-Commander) brought a bottle of brandy and we had speeches and toasts. Apparently he had hated us during the War but then he was captured and sent to a camp just outside London. An English family were very good to him, and he came to realise that he had been fighting for the wrong cause. As a result, he was now very friendly towards us. The German sailors had found us hostile, as I suppose we were at first, but then we asked them aboard and gave them a meal. It has always been the case that sailors all over the world make friends very easily and this was no exception.

There was to be a bread-making competition at Rosyth. The Captain had become interested and we were going to enter.

We arrived at Copenhagen and found the Aircraft Carrier *Bulwark* already there as well as the *Tyne* (a Submarine Depot Ship). We visited some breweries at Tuborg and Carlsberg. We were in six coaches, and our arrival caused quite a stir. We were shown round by guides who told us the history of the places. All the profits were given to the arts and science. They told us that in the first bottling department they normally bottled 1,500 bottles an hour, but with us lot they would have to work a double shift! Of course we all cheered.

Copenhagen is a beautiful city and I thoroughly enjoyed visiting it. My only reservation was the traffic. It had right of way over pedestrians and nipped along those wide streets at great speed. You really had to watch out for yourself. I managed to buy two small figurines in Danish national costume for Pauline. I went to a club – quite an élite place as it turned out – and fell into conversation with the pianist, who spoke good English. I found myself popular simply because I was English. Two Danish officers asked me to their table and bought me a beer. They too spoke excellent English. They seemed to like the Queen and also to be in favour of English good manners. They asked me what the English thought of Denmark. They seemed not to like Americans, though. Some Danish officers who had just passed through college would be making a return visit to us tomorrow.

The Cookery Officer had by this time transferred to the *Tidereach*, a Fleet Oil Tanker, as he couldn't find room for improvement on us. The *Tyne* was a terrific size and, of course, manned by civilians. The *Bulwark* left the next day. She was on independent command and wouldn't be taking part in the exercises about to commence. The C.-in-C. was on the *Tyne* and we were in line ahead with ourselves next and then *Tidereach*. We met some French ships too. Later we joined up with all kinds of other ships: two Carriers, a Dutch Cruiser and several more. The projected exercises in gun- and torpedo-firing had to be postponed due to fog, but we had what was called an ABCD exercise (Atomic, Biological, Chemical Defence), which in practice entailed wearing gasmasks and staying below the waterline. The flare that was supposed to represent the atomic bomb dropped straight on us, so we didn't take much part in the exercise itself apart from making a lot of smoke. The wind rose to gale force but fortunately it was blowing astern of us, so that it was less rough than it might have been. We then oiled from the *Tidereach*, an operation which could be dodgy in heavy seas. This Tanker was of the most recent type and was capable of refuelling five ships at once. The *Glasgow* was actually refuelling astern of us, with the Dutch ship, *Seven Provinces* on the port side and ourselves on the starboard. The two Carriers didn't have to re-fuel.

We passed Scapa Flow and were truly in Scottish waters. Short weekend leave was granted at Rosyth, but only to those whose homes were in the North and so far as our branch was concerned, that meant only the Chief and Lynn.

While we were still at sea, we had a sort of rehearsal for the baking competition, making some coburgs and cottage loaves. On the last night, as soon as we got in, we started storing ship and it was 10 p.m. before we had finished work. Since the butcher was also engaged in storing, we had to butcher the meat ourselves. We were alongside the *Glasgow* and had to go on board her and over her gangway – a five-minute walk just to spend a penny. The canteen too was very crowded, and there were no less than eight waiting to use the phone. When at last I got my turn it took 20 minutes to get through and even then I could hardly hear.

A day or two later an Admiral, Supply came into the after galley. For an Admiral he was quite nice and spoke to each of us in turn. He asked me how long I had had my rate and seemed to think I was quite young. Then he wanted to know whether I would be signing on again. He was quite pleased with everything.

We discovered that the baking competition was to be judged the following morning but the bread had to be sent in that afternoon, with the result that I could not enter.

That afternoon another Admiral came aboard, this time the FOFH or Flag Officer Flotillas of the Destroyers and Smaller Craft of the Home Fleet. He too was impressed and when he had finished he Cleared Lower Deck and gave us high praise for our conduct in general, plus efficiency and cleanliness inside and out. He also wished us all a happy leave and asked us to remember him to all our sweethearts and wives – a bit of a lad really, but I couldn't remember his name. A P.O., who had known him years before as a Captain, told me a story about him. If you went in front of him for punishment, he used to ask you: 'If I give you punishment, who will suffer?' If you said it would be your wife, he used to let you off. That was during the War, when wives did indeed suffer if their husbands' leave was stopped and also if their pay was docked. Nowadays, of course, the wife's allowance is not touched. The ship's company of the *Glasgow* were told (though we on the *Defender* were not as yet) that all Writers, Stores, Cooks, Stewards and S.B.As below the rank of P.O. would have to change into square rig and that this had to be completed within the next four years.

We had moved into the Basin, not far from the Forth Bridge, and were due to sail for Dover, arriving there on 27th July. There was just time to fit in a very brief leave before we sailed for the Belgian coast. Early the following morning we moved into Ostend Harbour, ready to pick up the King of Iraq. The Duke of Gloucester was representing the Queen.

King Faisal came aboard at 8.10 and we sailed almost immediately. Someone said that he was not a very big chap. If he pulled his socks up, he would blindfold himself.

We had an escort consisting of a Destroyer and two Frigates, which we met outside the Harbour, and we fired a 21-gun Salute. Also at Dover the Coastal Command did a fly-past and the Shore Battery there gave another 21-gun Salute. We arrived at Dover about 12.30. The Duke of Gloucester came aboard and the King and he left together. Everything went very well and we moved back into our old place. We did not splice the mainbrace, though!

CHAPTER IX

Changes on the Horizon

WE WERE DUE TO de-ammunition on the 23rd July at Sheerness and go to sea for half an hour before proceeding up the Medway to Chatham. I heard that the Captain had sent a signal to the Admiralty asking permission for wives and families to come aboard the following day at Sheerness. The Admiralty gave their approval but laid down that only one relation or friend would be allowed. If possible, I intended to put Pauline down for a pass, but if it turned out that I couldn't, it wouldn't be the end of the world. The relatives were to be picked up by the ship's boats at Cornwallis Jetty and brought on board. The arrangement was that we would then go to sea for a half-hour tour, after which we would be turning up river to Chatham, having had lunch on board. The whole thing would take about three and a half hours. I was off watch at the time too, so it would have been highly convenient, but unfortunately Pauline could not get the day off.

The D.O. asked me once more whether I had definitely decided not to sign on. If I did, he told me, I would pass my P.O.'s course on my papers alone. Naturally, my answer was 'no', and then he said; 'I have no doubt whatever that you will have an excellent report and that you will get on very well, just as you have in the Service.'

Derby's court case was due in Middlesborough on 26th or 27th September, but when it came to it, he was fined only £3.10. All the same the Captain gave him 14 days' stoppage of leave. He asked the D.O. if he could have three hours ashore and permission was granted, but he came back drunk and then, of course, he was in the rattle again and the Captain gave him another 14 days on top of the first lot. I thought that if he didn't pull himself together soon, he would find himself losing his rate. We got into Sheerness and commenced de-ammunitioning and the rest of our programme. The following day we would be at sea on trials. Immediately after this we would be ammunitioning again and then, late in the afternoon, sailing for Invergordon. As it turned out, it was blowing a gale outside which delayed us, and it was gone 10 p.m. by the time we had got back to Sheerness and dropped anchor. After nine weeks in the Dockyard, the gale shook some of the hands up! However, everything went all right with the trials.

Having ammunitioned, we made up for lost time and set sail in good weather for Invergordon, bowling along at a steady cruising speed.

While we were still at Invergordon, I had what could have turned out quite a nasty accident. I was walking down aft with a dish of meat when I slipped and nearly went over the side. I got covered in blood from the meat, but none of it came out of the dish. All the same it knocked the wind out of me!

At this time we had quite a few ships with us: some American and a Dutch Cruiser, though we had no Norwegians this time. We were due to go to sea on Wednesday morning and return on Friday. Pauline and I were still anxious about finding somewhere to live, and the subject kept cropping up in our letters to each other. The situation was made even more anxious while we were at Invergordon, where, for some reason, the mail was failing to get through. I still managed to get the galley painted even though that was really a job that the Seamen are supposed to do.

The next day we made an early start for the open sea and by 6.30 a.m. we were firing everything as well as doing a submarine-tracking exercise. We were due to fire the torpedoes that afternoon but the swell was too heavy and they would not risk it. Firing them was not the problem, but getting them back. Many were feeling too queasy to eat and I was the only one in our mess who enjoyed the veal and ham pie. We were due to oil ship the following morning, after spending the night at anchor, and then to do exercises until the late afternoon, returning to our buoy at Invergordon at 6.30 p.m. That would make it too late for any mail. The next day was not so bad though the wind was still strong. We turned so often that you really had to hang on. Just as the weather was at its worst, they piped all hands to dinner. It always seemed to happen like that! By this time it was getting much colder and we could see snow on the mountains. At last some mail arrived and a tape recording from Pauline. Unfortunately the tape-recorder in the mess worked at the wrong speed for this and I couldn't make it out. I saw one of the P.O.'s and he said he would let me use the ship's one, which had three speeds.

We went to sea for a gunnery practice before putting in to Rosyth. Captain's Rounds went very well again but Derby had a row with the Chief Cook, with the result that he was due to be transferred to the after galley to work with me. He certainly did get argumentative at times and was probably frustrated by having so much leave stopped. Anyway, some time later the Chief relented and allowed him to stay in the forrard galley.

I was still uncertain as to when I would be able to begin my civilian life. It depended on when Eden decided to call off the Emergency (the Suez

Crisis). I was sure, however, that we should press on with our arrangements for a new home; everyone believed that the crisis would not last long.

I heard the tape at last and found it very good. Pauline was much more confident and fluent on it than I. The P.O. who managed to make it work supplied me with earphones, so it remained private between Pauline and myself.

I was also trying to find out the exact date when I would be finishing, and confirmed with the Captain's Secretary that it would be 28 days before the 7th April, which, allowing for leave, would mean about the 10th March, 1957.

We had a busy gunnery agenda one morning but got mixed up with a fishing fleet and then the smaller guns destroyed a target being towed by a plane before the larger ones could have a go at it. Anyway, we had some fun trailing a fly plane behind and planes were going round firing flares and dropping a type of phosphorus bombs. I watched them for half an hour.

There was still no sign of Love, who, you remember, had failed return from shore leave. I was hoping not to see him again. I heard from a shipmate that his wife had found a letter from a girl in Stockholm, and we all thought that that was where he was. Much later I heard that he had been brought back under escort and would be under arrest. He would certainly get not less than ninety days and some believed that he would get six months. In the end we heard what fate had been decided for him when the Captain cleared Lower Deck and told us that he had been sentenced to ninety days in Edinburgh Prison and discharged from the Navy in Disgrace. So that was the last we would ever see of him.

One day the D.O. asked me how things were going at home and how Pauline was keeping. It was nice of him and I had noticed that he always asked after us when he thought about it. He never liked Derby, though, and was always sarcastic to him.

One night it was about 11 p.m. before we anchored, and the following night we went to sea again and took part in a really major exercise, firing at a remote-controlled plane. We smashed it to bits with the third shot! Later on we did some more firing at remote-controlled boats but this time failed to sink any. Just as well in a way; they cost thousands, I believe. I may mention that X-Gun Turret 4.5 Twin (the one aft) was just above my galley and that every time it fired, the blast smashed exactly the same three lights in it. In the course of these exercises a shell became jammed in the breach, and when that happened the correct practice was to fire it into the sea. That is, provided everything else was all right. At the time when this was going on I happened to be in the heads, and the barrels were lowered to a point just a scuttle behind me ready for firing into the sea. There I was reading a newspaper when bang! The thing blew out two lamps half an inch thick as well as smashing the bulbs. The glass was showering down and I was shaking it out of my pants. I wasn't cut at all, but it certainly shook me up and put me right off. After all that we returned thankfully to harbour, where I received an overdue pile of mail.

In further exercises we had all the guns banging away and X-Turret shot the sleeve down again. Then we went alongside the *Tidereach* to re-fuel and, having completed our part in the exercise, proceeded to Rosyth accompanied by *Daring* and *Glasgow*. We found ourselves alongside the *Daring*, with *Barleycorn* and *Barcarole* opposite. But there would not be anyone I knew on board after such a long time, so there was no point in paying her a visit. Then, just as I had made up my mind on this, one of my old shipmates from the *Barcarole* did come to see me, but too late for me to share my tot with him. Anyway, we decided to go and share his with him the next day.

Pauline and I got into the way of sending recording tapes to each other and it worked pretty well.

From Rosyth we sailed for Hamburg, which meant picking up a pilot at the mouth of the Elbe and going a long way up river to this inland city. It was to be my last trip abroad, since the only other one I would be making would be to Derry, or so I thought at the time. Later my expectations on this point were to be shattered. On the way up the Elbe we passed Cookshaven, which is quite a large industrial area in itself. We arrived on time and secured to a pontoon more or less in the middle of the stream but quite near the city. From there a wooden bridge led on to the road. Wherever you looked there were towering cranes, floating drydocks and ships in all stages of construction. The place was bustling with activity twenty-four hours a day. Some venues ashore were placed out of bounds owing to the danger of contracting V.D.

I had done a good amount of dhobying on the way over and I pressed, ironed and laid out all the clothes I would need. But the currency arrived late and in the end I felt it was all too much trouble to go ashore. I received some of the letters which I knew Pauline had sent, but not all. I supposed the rest would eventually catch up with us.

I mentioned before having met a number of German sailors at Kiel. Two of them came aboard one morning and that night they took a couple of our lads ashore with them. One of them came back with an unusual novelty – a bierstein. When he next went ashore, he brought me one back for Pauline. Later I went ashore myself and got some more of these for other members of the family.

After galley. Love, 'Pinky' and myself.

My veg. hand was nicknamed 'Pinky'. He had got into some kind of trouble ashore and had smashed a sign or a glass panel of some kind. He was put on a charge for this. But one man was on a truly terrible charge: attempted rape. He was on board but the civilian police were proceeding with his case. It was thought that he might get as much as seven years. He said he didn't remember a thing about it. The German beer was certainly strong. Some of the lads were coming back in an awful state.

Hamburg had by now been cleared of the terrible damage done in the War. Large clearings could be seen everywhere with the roads and footpaths running through. Building work was going on everywhere and in the shops the furniture was all modern-looking and contemporary, though decidedly smart. Messerschmitt and Lambretta scooters could be seen everywhere. Anyone discovered crossing the road against the lights could be summoned on the spot.

Pinky, my veg. hand, who had broken a glass panel, went back and paid for it as soon as he could and somehow the owners of the bar where it had happened seemed to take to him and friendly relations developed between them. I had a pleasant time too. I met a very agreeable couple. The man had been in the American Army for five years, but had had to leave when he decided to try and find his mother in the Eastern Zone. He got a job with the American Consul in Hamburg but lost it when he tried to contact his mother. However, he had just signed a contract to make records here and was celebrating this piece of luck. We got back about midnight after a thoroughly enjoyable evening.

A couple of days later we sailed for Ireland. The ship's office informed me that I was on top of the roster for a furnished flat and gave me a form to complete. I filled it in and returned it to the D.O.

As soon as we left the Elbe we ran into a force 8 gale and a real up-and-downer it was too. Many of the ship's company were really ill – largely due to the quantity of beer they had drunk the night before. The *Daring* was right behind us and as we watched her she seemed to lift out of the water and slide either to port or starboard.

That afternoon I was busy drawing and preparing the turkeys – no joke at the best of times, but even worse in the sort of weather we were experiencing. Then we prepared the brussels sprouts, though they were like marbles, and by the time we had done 300 of them we were getting pretty fed up. By 7 p.m. the hammocks were already going up. We had what we used to call the 'Green Baize' Club for those who wrote home regularly. We used to put a piece of green baize down on the table and write on that, and we all had a diamond-shaped piece as our club badge. Two of us used to write home every night and we were the secretaries. If one of the others missed a night, we used to have a council. When one hand failed to turn up three nights running, we threatened to write to his wife and tell her he had been dancing. She had threatened to shoot him if he did!

The night that we left the Elbe and headed out to sea in the gale, I found myself all alone at the green baize, which meant that some wives at least wouldn't be getting a letter. But the next night it was too rough even for me and I missed writing my nightly letter to Pauline. I was all right except for a terrible headache, which was quite enough to put me off the task of writing.

We were rolling pretty heavily all day and when it came to it, only four of us had any turkey, and as there was plenty, we scoffed the others' shares as well.

In the afternoon the Lieutenant announced over the tannoy that the Captain would be speaking to us. 'I have received the following top-secret signal,' he said. 'We are to make maximum speed to Malta with the *Daring*.'

There we were, then, steaming like mad for the Mediterranean. That afternoon, just off the Isle of Wight, we re-fuelled from *Tidereach*. We would be passing Gibraltar without stopping and still had no real idea of our final destination. All we knew was that we would be arriving at Malta on the following Wednesday. Some of the men and most of the officers had arranged to meet their wives in Londonderry and all these plans were, of course, completely scuppered. At the speed we were going – 28 knots – the vibration was too great for us to do much, and we still had to pass through the Bay of Biscay.

The Captain cleared Lower Deck and told us that he still had no information for us as to why we were bound for Malta and that he would not know until he reported to the C.-in-C. there. Lynn had been doing the baking and making horrible mistakes at it, with the result that the bread was dreadful. So the D.O. decided to change us round and I was baking from then on. I still believed that we would pay off on the date stipulated, so that our plans would not be affected. The paying off could be either at Chatham or at Malta itself; they could easily fly us home from there. We passed the *Apollo* and she sent us a signal, 'See you at Easter'. Then the C.-in-C. sent us another: 'You will do as well out there as you have here.' I knocked back two doughs that I had already made and they turned out smashing. I intended to make another about 9 p.m. that evening.

Plans were altered and we stopped at Gibraltar after all to pick up an officer and six ratings for passage to Malta. Another point that was a bit perplexing was what to wear now that the warmer weather was coming. No one on board had any whites, and I had been using mine in the galley. Another point was that we would be out of stores, except for the emergency ones, and would have to use tinned potatoes and other vegetables. Even with these, we would only just manage.

Later the D.O. came in and told me that there could be as many as thirty joining us to take passage to Malta. That meant that I would have to bake more bread. We stopped at Gibraltar about 1 a.m. that same night. Meanwhile the *Daring* carried on; she had already received mail by jackstay while at sea, whereas we would be getting ours at Gibraltar. However, we never went into the harbour. A boat came out to us bringing a Diving Team consisting of an Officer, a Chief P.O., two P.O.'s and fifteen Divers. Later on we heard what became of them once they reached Malta. They got organised there and two of them had already arranged to have their wives out. Then they started to move them around Malta. Next, all of a sudden, they found that no one wanted them and they were sent to Gibraltar to go home. The following day they were told that a ship would pick them up, yet they still did not know where they were going until they actually got on board. We could receive signals but not send any. That is real security for you!

The boat took our mail but the security regulations meant that it would be held up until we arrived at Malta. One of Pinky's pals got news that his mother had died and the poor lad was flown home from Gibraltar.

I had been in the galley for 48 hours and had developed an infection in my finger, so I had to have it lanced and Derby took over the baking. Four Russian Destroyers passed us and asked who we were and where we were going. The Captain must have enjoyed being able to ignore them. The Rock was signalling like mad when we came in that night but we just stopped and let them work it out. We still did not know what tasks we would be set on arrival. We were due to enter Malta Grand Harbour at 6 a.m. and then move out by 4 p.m. after taking on fuel, provisions and ammunition. To judge from the radio news, the Government must have known some time beforehand what was going to happen in the Canal Zone and what Israel would be doing, and that was why we had had our signal.

I had a thoroughly lazy day, because the Doc. still would not let me go back to work with my finger, which he had lanced. So I took a book on to X Gun Deck for most of the morning and basked in the sun. There was to be no shore leave when we arrived in Malta, so no one was bothering about whites any longer.

The next day I was back at the baking, the ship having arrived in Grand Harbour about 6 a.m. After ammunitioning, provisioning, watering and fuelling, we set sail again the same day for Suez. I had received a wonderful pile of mail – seven letters and a tape from Pauline and two others from other members of the family. I even managed to get the Naval Tailor to send flowers to Pauline on her birthday. My letters to her would have to be censored, but later I found that they had duly arrived on the 8th November, 1956.

Even then we did not know what task we would be given. We were issued with lifebelt, anti-flash gauntlets and balaclava, as well as tin hats, and were kept at our Action Stations. We had to carry our lifebelts around with us, which was a damned nuisance. Everything was battened down and we had deadlights on the scuttles and darkened ship every night. On the upper deck I couldn't see a thing. We were in Third Degree Readiness, as it was called, with someone at Action Stations all the time. I was just writing to Pauline when the alarm bell went. Don't you just move when it is the real thing! It took us less than a minute before we were all Closed up for Action Stations. The next time it happened I was at the pictures, and with one big rush, the place was cleared in seconds. Each time it turned out to be a false alarm. The next thing that happened was that one of our ships, coming from Cyprus, failed to give the daily call signal (which was changed every day) and nearly got shelled. On yet another occasion enemy aircraft were reported, but never came within range.

Our job, as it turned out, was to shield the Carriers, which meant that we were constantly tearing round the ocean. We were also acting as Pick-up Destroyer, as it is called. We used to steam behind a Carrier in case any plane overran the flight deck, in which case we would have picked up the pilot.

I spent some time watching the planes taking off and landing but they knew their job and all landed safely. However, one pilot had to circle five times before he could get down. The day of the Landing the Medical Officer was taken off by helicopter, and he spent two days in Port Said. When he came back he gave us an account of some of the things he had seen. The Egyptians had sunk everything they could in the Canal. To clear it would be a major operation, but apparently the work had already started.

There was a small armada off Port Said and in our Task Force we had a French Carrier as well as two of our own. Sometimes we got bread delivered to us by helicopter, which meant that we did not have to bake that particular night. We were all becoming bored with doing nothing. We had a dart board and we all used to 'cane' it until we got fed up and would then play cards or read. We had had no mail for nearly ten days.

We were probably about 30 miles from Port Said itself and hadn't had an actual sight of land since arriving. We heard on the wireless that our troops were leaving the Canal, so we knew the war wouldn't last much longer. There was something wrong with one of the Carriers, the one that kept us supplied with bread. She went funny with us and we got only enough bread for one supper. That meant that I had to turn to and bake that night.

The next day was Remembrance Day but I was too busy in the galley to get to the service. We took on some potatoes from a Supply Ship that morning and also re-fuelled from a Tanker. We had a copy of *The News of the World* on board and saw that the Egyptians had claimed to have sunk one of our Destroyers. Needless to say, there was not a grain of truth in it. I believe the *Diana* was at the other end of the Canal on her way home from the Far East and she did see some action, but she was certainly not sunk. We were due to leave as soon as the Police Force from the United Nations arrived. We had been at sea for 17 days without a break and would be glad of some rest.

A Frigate came alongside and transferred mail to us and I was lucky again. It meant that I would have to get cracking; some of Pauline's letters could be 26 pages long. Apparently, the reason that the Carrier could not supply us with sufficient bread was that she was supplying several Destroyers as well. We went alongside *Albion* one morning to collect bread and it seemed as though every time this happened, she would play rock and roll. So our Captain sent a signal: 'It's loaves we want, not rocks or rolls'!

We came to Port Said but anchored some distance away. The postman went ashore with an armed guard but there had still been no mail, although the bread arrived all right. We found the newspapers that were sent very interesting, as we certainly did not know about the demonstrations in London.

By this time we were at sea again and hoping that we would soon be departing for Malta. Meanwhile we put into Port Said for a Self-Maintenance. We re-fuelled there and then returned to our station in the Task Force. By this time mail was flowing better. We anchored just in the mouth of the Canal at Port Said and started our Self-Maintenance. The fresh water was certainly a problem, and the machinery would have to be out of action for some time. They had closed down the fresh water showers and rigged up salt water ones instead.

Now that I was working in the afternoons, I was no longer baking and had no veg. hand and no butcher. They were both in Defence Watches. By this stage we were due to sail the next day, arriving on the 25th November, 1956. I had heard on the News that the Reservists would be released, and concluded that even now my release would have come through by March.

We made a collection for the Hungarian Relief Fund and managed to raise £100 out of our welfare fund, which included £6 from our mess – not bad for only nine of us!

Fresh water was being rationed since we were using a lot for the boilers, so the bathroom was open only at certain hours. All the time we were working in a criss-cross course and kept the same distance from the coast throughout.

CHAPTER X

H.M.S. *Calton*, My Last Ship

WE ARRIVED IN MALTA on 25th November, 1956. I found a bumper mail waiting for me, with numerous newspaper cuttings and magazines. A shipmate was flying home next day and I hoped he would post my letters from Stanstead. I went to Valetta and bought a present for Pauline's birthday and afterwards met the Chief Cook. We both had 'big eats' and a few jars together afterwards. He was staying ashore so I came back on board. At that time it looked as though I would be home on the Thursday, Friday or Saturday, and I was really only waiting for my relief to arrive. Then I found out that we would be going to Chatham first. I had left my suitcase at home and was finding it difficult to know how to pack all my kit with so little space. We were in four Watches by this time, and there was no more baking to be done. The people who were recommissioning – about ninety of them – were flying home. We hoped to leave on the same planes as our reliefs would be arriving on.

My letters were gradually catching up with me from Port Said. The Mess sent birthday greetings to Pauline. Derby would not put his name on the card because he felt that she didn't like him. She should worry! I cleaned up my overcoat and packed the biersteins I had got in Hamburg in preparation, but what I was going to do with the rest of my gear I just didn't know. By this time the ship was flying the paying-off pennant, though it was so long that most of it was in the harbour.

I flew home on the 30th and on arrival at Paddington, phoned Pauline at her work place. Then I went on to Chatham for seven days' leave documents, arriving back in London and so to Eastcote by about 12 midnight, December 4th. Pauline came down to Chatham and we had a look at a married quarters house in Gillingham. It had a large detached conservatory, with light windows – very promising, we thought. By the 17th we had obtained the keys, and we moved down on the 19th, staying the night at the NAAFI Club. Over Christmas I was on Duty Watch in Barracks, so it was the 27th December before we moved.

On the 9th February I joined the *Calton*, a minesweeper, at Portsmouth. I did all I could to stay at Chatham but no joy! I was told that there was a shortage of Leading Cooks with sea experience and had to go. We decided

H.M.S. Calton.

to give up the house in Gillingham and moved most of our gear to Eastcote before catching the train to Portsmouth. During the weekend I moved up to Leicester and signed up for a bungalow.

I had thought that I would never need to write again, but found myself writing my first letter from Portsmouth on the 9th February, 1957. Pauline had seen me off at the station.

I arrived a little after midday and took a taxi straight to the ship, which was lying at Vernon dockyard. None of the officers was on board so I reported to the Duty P.O. and gave him my draft papers. The ship was smaller than *Barcarole* and had only four officers and a total complement of 29 to cook for. The officers used to get the same food as the hands. She was only two years old and her equipment throughout was modern. She had bunks and folding tables, and even inserts for bedding in the bulkheads. The galley was really smashing and I had never seen one so well equipped, what with the electric range and all the gadgets. I had a mincing machine, a slicer, spud-peeler – all electric, so that I could fix them up to do almost anything. They were all in stainless steel and the benches were wooden. What a difference from the Bar boats!

A Seaman had been doing the cooking and he said he would do the supper that night so that I could settle in. He would also help me the following day. He wanted to get measured for a suit, so I took over for him and tidied up while he went for this. Then he took over again.

A few days later we went to sea and would be away all week, working by day and anchoring at night. I foresaw that mail could be awkward. Many of the hands had hobbies which they practised on board. One of the stokers in the mess was making a model plane and another a ship. Someone else was doing marquetry and had just bought a kit to make a picture out of strips of various kinds of wood. I found out that two of them were doing this. When they had completed it and polished it, it looked extremely smart. I showed them my old painting set and said I would be getting my rug out soon. I did do a bit of work on it a few evenings later, but I still had a long way to go. As things worked out, I could never find time to do much on it.

The next morning I did both breakfast and lunch and everyone told me how much they enjoyed them. They also said that the cook before me had been rotten. Apparently the Captain had sent a signal asking for a Leading Cook who was immune to sea-sickness, but I was also told that this ship, being made of alloy and having only a six-foot draught, rolled quite a bit. So my years of being free from sea-sickness were to be changed.

The electric range was a beauty and built up to a great heat very quickly. I also had an electric heater for water and tea. I did some dhobying and hung it in the galley. I believed we were due back in Portsmouth on Friday afternoon. There was some talk of the ship paying off in the next four weeks or so. She had been brought out of reserve because of the Suez crisis.

After a few days we left harbour at 10.00 hours and ran straight into rough weather off the Isle of Wight. For the first time I was sea-sick. The movement of this little ship upset me and was I mad! Next morning the First Lieutenant came into the galley and shook hands. He said he understood that since I came aboard the food had improved considerably. Then the Captain came to see me and asked one or two questions – quite a decent chap, I thought, but time would tell. All the hands seemed to think he was quite good. I judged this to be a hardworking little ship. The Seamen had been up in the rain and wind all day.

The ship seemed not bad but oh how she did roll – like a cork! You wouldn't chuckle! Three parts of her were above water and she was almost top-heavy. The alloy of which she was built was too light for stability, and in bad weather nothing much could be done. Next morning we were at sea again by 6.30. We certainly did not waste much time!

I found that we were the senior vessel out here out of five. Four more officers came aboard and one had already come before we left, which made ten, including one Canadian. The number I was cooking for was now 35. I was certainly being kept busy. In fact it was difficult to find time to write and in any case the ship was rolling too heavily. We did not get in until after 9 p.m.

Everyone seemed pleased with my efforts and the Captain, a Lieutenant-Commander, asked if I was all right. He made favourable comments on all the meals and one day gave me a bottle of beer. The First Lieutenant said he had never eaten so well. Apparently the last cook used to go flat out at sea. By this time I had just about got used to the motion of the ship, even though the weather was still not all that good. The weekends were not too bad. I used to do a duty one week, then have a long weekend, and then a short one. All leaves expired on Mondays at 07.30. I asked for a long weekend to enable me to get to Leicester.

Our task was to find mines dropped by another ship, sweep for them when they came to the top, and then shoot them and sink them. One night we continued sweeping until 2 a.m. in the morning, and every morning I had to be up really early. Sometimes the weekenders didn't get away till 5 p.m. We were told that we would be returning to Chatham on 22nd. Just a few weeks to go and they had sent me to sea again! I thought I had said goodbye to that life for good and being sea-sick at the very end of my Naval career was not pleasant. I certainly felt I should not like being at sea in a minesweeper of this sort for any considerable time.

One of the seamen on board used to read the Bible every morning – funny type of chap but pleasant enough. I told him of my trip to Nazareth and he was very interested. One night the Steward went ashore, so I served supper for them – as if I hadn't enough to do! – and the Captain asked about Pauline. I told him about her move from Gillingham.

The next day we went to sea for what looked like being a long day with a late finish. We took 19 Sub-Lieutenants with us for training, but they brought their own food, which was just as well. The following night I fried fish and chips for supper and served in the Wardroom again, but this time there was only the Midshipman on board. Next morning we had thick fog but went out just the same. It didn't clear and we were forced to anchor, so we came back during the afternoon.

The baker failed to come one morning, though he had promised to do so. (Actually we just managed on what we had got). I got on the phone next door and gave them a blast, telling them that if it happened again, we would change to a different baker. They sent the bread right away! Then I phoned the butcher and gave them a blast too – this time for too much fat in the stewing steak. All in all, I had quite a good time!

Although the galley was so fine, it still had to be cleaned and I also had to look after supplies such as milk (which was fresh), bread and other stores. I was forever ordering and used to spend pounds at a time – smashing! On the *Barcarole* all this used to be done by the Coxswain and Tanky. So in addition to being Chef, I had several other jobs to do as well, including that of Steward sometimes.

My pay still hadn't been worked out from R.N.B. and the first time I went ashore I only had £2.10s. I knew it would come right eventually, but I would have to wait until the following fortnight. I would just have enough to get to Leicester, and certainly couldn't spend any on runs ashore. In any case all I wanted was a haircut.

One day the Captain was painting a small grill on the Upper Deck which he called the chicken hut – actually it was some kind of exhaust casing, but I asked him whether the hens had laid! He saw some A/Bs on the *Caunton* doing nothing, so he shouted over to them: 'If you haven't got anything to do, come over here and we will find you some work.' One night, about 9 p.m., he brought his wife on board and asked me to do some tiddly sandwiches for her.

I asked him what she would like as we had some cold beef and ham on board but it turned out that she liked corned beef. Like a lot of the officers' wives, she was an American. The Captain promised me a bottle of beer when we got some aboard. He was quite good, the Skipper, and I used to get on with him fine. We also had a sort of mad skiffle group aboard called Geordie and his Vomits. The Captain brought them a hooter. We were thoroughly mad on the *Calton*. I asked the Chief Coxswain to arrange for me to see the Captain and he mentioned to the First Lieutenant that I wanted a reference. He said he would give me one and that he would type it out that afternoon. That night the First Lieutenant gave it to me and I sent it to Pauline, thinking she would like to see it.

Another day three R.N.R.'s joined us for a week, which meant three more mouths to feed. However I got along quite well and they seemed pleased. The other chef was still in *Vernon* and being treated at the hospital, but when I told the Seamen that he was coming back, they all shouted, 'We don't want him back.'

I went ashore with the Steward and we had a couple of pints but I felt I could never get used to Pompey – Chatham was my place. The next day we had Captain's Rounds, and he was pleased with the ship in general. *Caunton* moved into the Dockyard, which enabled us to move right up to the jetty with another minesweeper, the *Billington*, alongside us. I was able to phone Pauline from her. I had met her First Lieutenant in a bar in Malta when Pauline and I were out there together. It was quite a surprise to meet him again and we had a pleasant chat.

A day or two later we went to sea and expected to spend several days before getting back to Pompey. We had a training class with us. Fortunately the weather was not bad and the sea was calm. The following week the ship was due to pay off at Chatham and the ship's company, it was believed, would be taking over the *Billington* there. But then so many drafts began coming through that the ship's company seemed to be breaking up, and I couldn't see how they would take over another ship.

The Coxswain arranged for me to get away early and I spent a long weekend leave at Leicester, in the course of which we made all the necessary arrangements with our solicitor and building society. We also chose a firegrate, paint and paper. Later I organised a nameplate for the new bungalow. It was to be made on board by Bungy, the Killick stoker and would only cost me a couple of tots. He was finding it difficult to get the right wood, so one afternoon I took a walk over to the Chippies' Shop in *Vernon* and asked a Chief there whether he could fix me up. He trimmed up a smashing piece, 18" by about 4½", and when I asked him what I owed him, replied 'nothing'. He wouldn't even take a packet of cigarettes. Bungy sandpapered it and painted it golden brown. After two coats, he painted the name on in black letters and varnished it. The frame and glass had come from *Diligence*, the letters from Eastcote and the paint from Bungy himself. The first lot failed to dry properly so Bungy took it all off, painted it white, and covered it with a glass frame. It didn't cost me anything and in the end Bungy wouldn't accept so much as a tot. It lasted for years outside our house until it finally fell to pieces.

Although the draft notices were coming in steadily, mine still had not arrived. We were victualling only for a few days, after which the shore establishment would be taking over. Shrove Tuesday came round and I was very busy making pancakes. Then they told me that another six would be joining us for lunch, and, furthermore, that there would be an inspection that afternoon by the Captain of *Vernon*. What a day it was, but in the end it all sorted itself out.

My pay came through but all I got was £3, since I had already had £1 Casual earlier on. My full pay, I believe, came to £11, but with allotments and the allowance I had arranged to be paid to Pauline, my actual pay varied between £4 and £4.10s a fortnight. (When I went to work in a bakery, my pay for the first week came to £12, though I had to work longer hours than in the Navy.)

We finally left Portsmouth and arrived at Hythe at 2.30 in the afternoon. Here there was a real graveyard for ships – all minesweepers 'in mothballs'. We were on the end of a long pier and all around were ships asleep in reserve, all coated on their Upper Decks with some type of plastic. *Calton* would soon be among them. The following day we had to go to sea for engine trials, but only for half an hour. All those on board with a draft had had it cancelled until she had been turned over to Reserve. I believed mine would come some time in the following week. They would cease to eat on board from Wednesday onwards. My final task was to put the galley in preservation order and it would probably take me until the Friday to complete it.

At last my draft came through, though I was still under orders from the Captain, who told me that there was still too much to do and too much to put into storage for him to let me go yet. There was the equipment to return and the stainless steel to grease in the galley – I was going to be very busy. When I heard this, I asked for a weekend on draft. He wrote the signal out for me there and then. After completing my final tasks, I packed up all my kit. Then I wrote my last letter to Pauline from the *Diligence*. Later I discovered that for some unknown reason she had kept all my letters, and it is on these, as well as on our diaries, that this book is largely based.

On Monday, 18th March, 1957, I went back to Chatham, setting out at 5 a.m. in the morning. I was still not clear of work even then, as I was on duty and also duty weekend. On the 24th, a Thursday, I met Pauline and on the 27th we went to Waterloo. I went on to Woking for my civilian clothes and met Pauline at her office. We had lunch together and after that went back to Eastcote, where I changed into civvies. On the 28th we travelled to Leicester and the following day I started my new work.

AMEN!

Appendix

A Condensed Narrative of the Wartime Activities of the 'Defender' Class of Nine Destroyers

Compiled for the members of the 'D' Boats Association
by J.R. Gower

AT THE OUTBREAK OF WAR, in September 1939, the 'D' Boats were dispersed around the China Station between Shanghai and Singapore. *Duncan* was their leader.

Within two years of the Declaration of War seven out of nine had been lost. Was this an ill-fated flotilla? Only *Duncan* and *Decoy* were left and both survived the War. Many other flotillas were equally hard-hit. After all, we lost 176 Destroyers during the War. Yet some flotillas were lucky – the 'O' Class who formed the 17th D/F Home Fleet comes to mind. They saw much action between 1941 and 1945 in Arctic and North Atlantic waters, between them they steamed over one million nautical miles and never lost a ship, although a number were damaged.

No, the 'D's had a good name and reputation, emphasised by a repeat of their names in the Post-War 'Daring' Class. Here is their story in brief.

As soon as War was declared, the 'D's were ordered nearer home, to the Med., but later some were allocated to the South Atlantic Station. Those in the Med. even had hopes of Christmas at home. *Duchess* was one. She was escorting the *Barham* from the Med. to the Clyde when disaster struck. The two ships were in collision off the Mull of Kintyre on the 12th December and *Duchess* was sunk.

The next was *Daring*. She too had reached home waters and on 18th of February, while escorting a convoy from Norway, was torpedoed by a U Boat (U 23) off Duncansby Head. Her stern was blown off; she capsized and sank within 30 minutes. Five survivors were picked up by H.M.S. *Thistle* but 9 officers and 148 ratings were lost.

Diana was certainly home by April, as was *Delight*, as both took part in the Norwegian Campaign, in which over 160 R.N. ships were involved. I have no record of *Diana* throughout that long summer. Perhaps she was refitting for service in the R.C.N., in which she became the *Margaree* on 6th

September 1940. Alas, on the 22nd October 1940 she was rammed and sunk with heavy loss of life when her O.O.W. put her across the bows of SS *Fort Fairy*. Two ships already lost in collision. How true our Naval Prayer, in which we ask 'for protection from the dangers of the sea and the violence of the enemy'.

So next we turn to *Delight*. After refitting at Portsmouth she was on passage to the Clyde on July 29th 1940. Just off Portland, she was bombed by German aircraft, having been detected by their new R.D.F. at a range of sixty miles. 16 Ju 87s attacked her during the last dog watch. A forward fuel tank was ruptured and fires were raging. Luckily her cry for help on her portable wireless transmitter reached Portland and two Motor Launches and two M.A.S.B.s went to her rescue, arriving about 2100. *Delight* finally blew up about 2210. Luckily casualties were comparatively light. All officers were saved and 147 ratings landed, including one dead and thirty-three seriously wounded. This completes the losses for the first ten months of War: *Duchess – Daring – Diana – Delight*.

What about *Duncan*, our leader? She got home for Christmas and a refit at Chatham. As soon as she came out, she was holed in collision escorting convoy ON 8. No casualties. It earned her another six months in dock but no commendations! In October she escorted *Ark Royal* to Gibraltar, by which time the remaining four 'D's were back in the Med.: *Dainty*, *Diamond*, *Defender*, *Decoy*, based at Alexandria. Throughout the summer and autumn of 1940 they carried out the usual maid-of-all-work duties required of Destroyers, too numerous to mention. *Dainty*, *Decoy* and *Defender* however, were at the action off Calabria, escorting *Ark Royal* to bombard the Jardian airfields. *Diamond* was at the Fleet Air Arm attack on Taranto, and she, with *Defender* and *Duncan*, was at the Battle of Spartivento in November, escorting via Admiral Somerville in *Renown* with *Ark Royal* and a number of Cruisers when they fought off the Italian Fleet trying to interfere with our control of the Med. *Dainty* too had great success when with *Ilex* during June she sank two Italian Submarines – or was it three? So ends 1940.

1941 was to bring more sorrow. On 24th February *Dainty* was sunk by German aircraft off Tobruk. I have no details, so ex-*Dainty*'s may be able to fill in.

Diamond was next to follow on 27th April, again the result of attacks by German aircraft. At the start of the War *Diamond* came to the Med., but was allocated to the South Atlantic, where she operated from Freetown. But she was back in May, based at Alex. to form the 10th Destroyer Flotilla with five R.A.N. Destroyers. It was this that took her to Greece in April for the evacuation of Allied troops. Among the ships engaged was the SS *Slamat*, an unarmed Transport carrying over 1000 soldiers. On 27th of April she came under attack from German aircraft and was sunk. *Diamond* and *Wryneck* picked up 700 survivors and started for Crete, but they too came under air attack. Both were badly hit and sank immediately. From all three ships, only 1 officer, 41 ratings and 8 soldiers survived. Thus went a ship with 16 Battle Honours dating from the Armada in 1588.

Defender went next, another victim of German air attack, on 11th July. A near miss off Sidi Barrani caused an explosion just abaft the forward bulkhead of the Engine Room. The *Vendetta* in company took her in tow but she sank almost at once; fortunately there were no casualties. Both *Defender* and *Diamond* had been at the Battle of Cape Matapan earlier in the year, when Admiral Cunningham annihilated a number of the Italian Fleet and *Defender* had also survived the evacuation of Greece and then Crete. It was sad, therefore, for her to meet her end in a less hazardous operation when she had been through so much.

We are thus left with just two ships – *Duncan* and *Decoy*. *Decoy* had been damaged by aircraft on 29th May, but not seriously, and, like Defender, she had subsequently survived both evacuations, those of Greece and Crete. She was also with Admiral Vian at the first Battle of Sirte. Thereafter we have lost track of *Decoy* but she must have come home to be turned over to the R.C.N., for on the 12th April 1943 she became R.C.N. *Kootenay*. We will come back to her in her new role.

Let us now finish *Duncan*'s story. We left her in the Med., but based at the Western end of Gibraltar as a unit of the 13th D/F. On 1st January 1941 she was involved in the interception of a Vichy French convoy, then escort to the troop convoy through the Med., and then she screened Force H when they bombarded Genoa. On return, she screened *Repulse* and *Furious* to Freetown and stayed in that area until July and so back to the Med. By November she was back in Chatham for refit.

In February 1942 she screened *Malaya* out of Gib. and April found her in Durban, South Africa From there she sailed with *Devonshire* escorting a slow convoy for the occupation of Diego Suares, Madagascar (5th May). She was transferred to the 22nd D/F Eastern Fleet and was in Colombo in June. She was back in Freetown in October, whence she escorted the *Royal Sovereign* to Bermuda. Then to New York, back to Freetown and thence to Liverpool to join the Western Approaches Command. This was a terrific round trip. She was due for refit and went to London until March 1943 and then to Liverpool to join Escort Unit B7, a very busy group.

She was constantly in action with U Boats. This was the turn of the tide in the Atlantic, when the U Boats were being overcome and long-range aircraft were successfully bridging the gap. I record only her successes. In May 1943 *Duncan*, with the Corvette *Snowflake*, sank U 381 and in October she picked up 15 survivors from U 470, which had been sunk by Liberator aircraft. A fortnight later, with *Sunflower* and *Vidette*, they sank U 282. After this she had earned another refit and was back in the Thames by November. Was she a Chatham ship? If so, she was continually lucky with her refits.

She was back in service by July 1944 and re-allocated to the 14th Escort Group until June 1945, when she was reduced to reserve and scrapped at Barrow on the 8th July. After a slow start, *Duncan* had proved her worth and survived six years of war.

Finally let us examine *Decoy*'s record in the R.C.N. It was outstandingly successful. She formed part of the Invasion Forces on 'D' Day, then on 6th July 1944 *Kootenay*, *Ottawa* and *Statice* sank U 678 off Brighton. A month later, on 18th August, *Kootenay*, *Chaudiere* and *Ottawa*, all R.C.N., sank U 621 in the Bay of Biscay. Just two days later, on the 20th August, the same three ships sank U 984 off Ushant. What a wonderful record! Where did *Decoy* end her service? After much research, I discovered the answer to this question in an invaluable book by H.T. Lenton and J.J. Colledge entitled *Warships of World War Two*. '*Decoy* H75, Built Thornycroft 7-6-1932. Was transferred to the R.C.N. 1943 as *Kootenay* and was the last of the Class and was scrapped 1946. *Duncan* was scrapped 1945'.

Message from E.J. Horner, Founder Member of The D-Boats Association

Members of the Association. This is your War Record. You can be proud of it. Your combined Battle Honours testify to this.